D0196191

# BUSINESS GUIDE TO JAPAN
*A Quick Guide to Opening Doors and Closing Deals*

# BUSINESS GUIDE TO JAPAN

*A Quick Guide to Opening Doors and Closing Deals*

Boyé Lafayette De Mente

TUTTLE PUBLISHING

Tokyo · Rutland, Vermont · Singapore

Published by Tuttle Publishing, an imprint of Periplus Editions (HK) Ltd., with editorial offices at 364 Innovation Drive, North Clarendon, Vermont 05759.

Library of Congress Control Number: 2006924487

Previously published as *Businessman's Guide to Japan* © 1989

ISBN-10:  0-8048-3760-0
ISBN-13:  978-0-8048-3760-6

Distributed by:

North America,
Latin America & Europe
Tuttle Publishing
364 Innovation Drive
North Clarendon, VT 05759-9436
Tel: (802) 773-8930
Fax: (802) 773-6993
info@tuttlepublishing.com
www.tuttlepublishing.com

Asia Pacific
Berkeley Books Pte. Ltd.
130 Joo Seng Road
#06-01/03 Olivine Building
Singapore 368357
Tel: (65) 6280-1330
Fax: (65) 6280-6290
inquiries@periplus.com.sg
www.periplus.com

Japan
Tuttle Publishing
Yaekari Building, 3rd Floor
5-4-12 Ōsaki
Shinagawa-ku
Tokyo 141 0032
Tel: (03) 5437-0171
Fax: (03) 5437-0755
tuttle-sales@gol.com

09 08 07 06   10 9 8 7 6 5 4 3 2 1
Printed in Canada

TUTTLE PUBLISHING ® is a registered trademark of Tuttle Publishing, a division of Periplus Editions (HK) Ltd.

# CONTENTS

# BUSINESS GUIDE TO JAPAN

# PREFACE
*The "Smell and Taste" of Japanese Companies*

JAPAN IS ONE of the most lucrative consumer and industrial markets in the world. It is also one of the world's most challenging markets, requiring special knowledge and special talents as well as extraordinary commitment, patience, and persistence.

Japan's maverick author, consultant, and critic-at-large Michihiro Matsumoto says that the best way to understand how Japan's business world works—and to succeed in it—is to look at each company as a glob of *natto* (not-toe).

Natto is a traditional Japanese food made from fermented soybean paste. It looks terrible, smells awful, and to the unconditioned foreign palate tastes like a batch of glue gone bad. Until recent times, one of the ways the Japanese used to measure the commitment of foreigners to Japan was by whether or not they could eat natto. The question was not if they liked it, but whether they were able to eat it despite its taste and smell.

Matsumoto describes all Japanese organizations, political, professional, and social as well as

I

economic, as natto organisms, and he makes several points with his pungent analogy:

1. Japanese companies are quintessentially Japanese and are therefore unlike companies in any other country.
2. Japanese companies have a distinctive character and flavor that only the Japanese can fully understand and accept.
3. And, foreigners who have not acquired a "taste" and appreciation for Japanese companies over a long period of time will inevitably find them difficult to deal with.

Until the 1990s, one of the unique characteristics of Japan's natto companies was that few of them had permanently established, well-defined "doors" for letting in outsiders, whether businesspeople or the public at large. Each organization was more or less a gluey monolith that was difficult or impossible to penetrate using the typical, straightforward Western approach.

A great many of these natto characteristics are still discernible in most Japanese companies, including those with conspicuously Western images, and there has been little if any change. In many large older companies such adjustments are neither visible nor measurable in practical terms.

The examples of such high-profile companies as Nissan and Sony appointing foreign executives as CEOs and chairmen are rare exceptions that shake the still deeply embedded cultural roots of Japan's business community and government.

Generally, the only partial exceptions to Matsumoto's metaphorical image are new enterprises—usually small- to medium-size—that were founded by young entrepreneurial mavericks who broke all of the traditional rules. But the larger these entrepreneurial companies grow, the more "typically Japanese" they become.

Given these circumstances, there are still valuable lessons to be learned from the Matsumoto "handbook" on Japanese companies. He says that when an outsider who has no inside connections tries to establish a relationship with a company—in the hope of doing business—he almost never penetrates the outer wall of the castle.

When the outsider makes a cold approach to a company, its walls may "give" a little at the point of pressure, like a mushy balloon, and bulge out somewhere else, but no permanent break is made in the company ramparts.

Matsumoto maintains that the only way businesspeople—foreign or Japanese—can actually get through the protective "shell" of a company is for someone on the inside to pull them in. Again, there are conspicuous exceptions to this rule, but they are still rare.

If an outsider does manage to get inside the walls of a company with a project proposal—via an acceptable introduction with help from someone on the inside—and the company is in fact interested in the project, it proceeds to digest or "Japanize" the project to make it compatible with the whole corporate organism. This homogenizing process is not something that can be done quickly. In fact, it is often the straw that breaks the back of the impatient time and money-conscious foreign suitor.

Regardless of how far along Japanese companies might be in dispensing with their traditional natto characteristics, there are specific culturally sanctioned protocols for approaching and dealing with them that are as structured as mathematical equations. Generally, one cannot successfully establish contact and develop a business relationship with a Japanese company without following these protocols in the right order and in the right way.

On an individual, personal basis, the traditional attitudes and behavior of the Japanese have changed dramatically from the hidebound cultural patterns of the past to a mind-set that is as open and as pragmatic as that typical of Westerners · particularly among the young.

But in the adult business and professional world when these people interact with other Japanese as members of a group or team, they must conform to the existing culture of whatever organization they belong to—and that culture remains very much "Japanese" in the traditional sense.

This quick guide to doing business in Japan identifies key cultural factors that continue to be the basis for the nature of typical Japanese companies and provides insights and guidelines for approaching and dealing with them successfully.

Boyé Lafayette De Mente
Tokyo, Japan

# THE STRANGE BEDFELLOWS

THE FIRST KEY to understanding and dealing with Japanese businessmen is keeping in mind that there are two categories of culture—one that is visible and tangible and one that cannot be seen or touched. It is the invisible culture of Japan that sets the Japanese apart from other people and makes their way of doing business different and often difficult for others to understand and follow.

While Japan's invisible culture has been considerably diluted since the end of World War II in 1945—and continues to change—it remains the primary force in the Japanese political and economic systems.

Cultural differences that continue to distinguish Japanese businessmen from their American and European counterparts are basic and extend across the board, from their values and the nature of their human relationships to how they go about accomplishing things.

The foundation of Japanese beliefs and behavior is bound up in a series of key words that express their philosophy, describe their mind-set, and prescribe the way they do things. The bedrock word in Japanese behavior is *amae* (ah-my), which refers to an idealized relationship between people—one of absolute trust and benevolence in which no one takes undue advantage of the other and all are united in a philosophical and spiritual bond that transcends the mean and mundane.

The second most important word in the lexicon of the Japanese way is *wa* (wah), which means "peace and harmony," and which is both an outgrowth of amae and an essential ingredient for its existence and application. Of course, neither of these principles has ever worked perfectly, but they have been and still are the national ethic of the Japanese.

The whole fabric of Japanese culture that grew out of the philosophies of Shintoism, Buddhism, Confucianism, and Daoism was shaped and colored by the principles of amae and wa, in particular the etiquette and ethics of interpersonal relationships from the highest authority down to the lowest laborer. These relationships, and their psychological offspring, are what give the Japanese business system its form and much of its essence.

Other factors that have played primary roles in the molding of the Japanese character and greatly influenced the Japanese attitude toward foreigners and the way they conduct business are the small size of their homeland, its relative isolation from the rest of the world during most of their history, their racial homogeneity, their deeply held belief of the superiority of their way of wa, and—until recently—their view of the outside world as an enemy to be kept at bay at all costs.

With the forced opening of Japan to the West by the United States in the 1850s, the national character of the Japanese was made even more complex by the rapid development of an inferiority complex brought on by their sudden exposure to the material wealth and power of Western countries, which had been transformed by the Industrial Revolution.

This new psychological factor intermingled with the rest of their invisible cultural heritage, giving the Japanese a kind of split personality—strong feelings of superiority on one hand and equally strong feelings of inferiority on the other hand. This combination of feelings was to have a profound influence on the subsequent history of the Japanese and continues today to affect all of their attitudes and behavior toward foreigners, in personal as well as business relationships.

While there are a growing number of Japanese who have been internationalized to the point that they can think like, talk like, and behave like Westerners, they are still the exception, and when dealing with fellow Japanese, they must submerge their "international self" and conform to the all-encompassing "Japanese way"—or find themselves even more isolated and often at as great a disadvantage as many Westerners who have chosen to live and work in Japan. While amae and wa are no longer absolute values, they remain the philosophical and ethical foundations of Japanese conduct.

Probably the second most important key in dealing effectively with the Japanese is an understanding of the emotional factor in their makeup.

# THE CULTURE OF EMOTION

PART OF THE OLD stereotype of the Japanese was that they were both inscrutable and unemotional. As it turns out, the Japanese are easier to know than most other people because their mind-set is far more precisely structured and homogenized than that of most. And as for regarding the Japanese as unemotional, that mistake has been the downfall of many an insensitive foreigner, not to mention the cause of a lot of trouble on the international front.

The Japanese are, in fact, far more emotional than Americans and most other Westerners, again for very solid historical reasons.

Most Westerners are used to a degree of frankness, candid criticism, slights, and outright insults and have developed a thick skin to counter such behavior. Most Westerners are also practiced in giving as good as they get. Not the Japanese. Their cultural conditioning has been to totally avoid such behavior, to keep such a tight rein on their emotions that people would not know what they were thinking or feeling, especially in formal and business situations.

This, of course, was the origin of the Western perception of the Japanese as unemotional. But beneath their calm front, the Japanese seethe with unrequited emotions. Their highly refined etiquette system, especially in the use of the "proper" level of language to each individual, makes them extremely sensitive to the most subtle of slights or unsanctioned behavior. Their skin is so thin and they are so sensitive that a brief look of disapproval flickering across a person's face may be enough to devastate them or earn their undying wrath.

This sensitivity and the bottling up of normal human emotions over the centuries resulted in the Japanese being prone to extreme violence when they found themselves free of the restraints and rules of their culture, especially in war and in dealing with captives and criminals. Historically, there have also been examples of individuals suddenly snapping and engaging in extreme behavior because they simply couldn't take it anymore.

In the 1950s when hordes of Japanese businessmen began going abroad on study and survey trips, many of them became so stressed out that they became ill within a few days and either returned to Japan immediately or stayed in their hotel rooms until they were scheduled to go home.

In the following years, whenever possible, Japanese companies opened branches abroad to handle all of their foreign operations because they only felt comfortable and secure when dealing with other Japanese.

Part of the emotional makeup of older Japanese involves a resentment factor that is a holdover from their history. There has always been a deep-seated belief among the Japanese that foreigners, Westerners in particular, look down on them and take advantage of them whenever they can.

Japanese skin is now much thicker than what it was as late as the 1980s, but it is still gossamer thin when compared to the typical American or European. Their emotional antennae are up and on twenty-four hours a day, especially in their dealings with non-Japanese.

The problem of their emotional sensitivity is compounded where foreigners are concerned—except when the foreigners are in the "honored guest" category—because as much as they may try, most un-internationalized Japanese readily

12

admit that associating with foreigners makes them uncomfortable.

Still today, franker businessmen privately admit that they do not like dealing with foreigners and would not do business with them if they had a choice—a cultural response that results from the fact that they cannot predict the behavior of foreigners and find much of it displeasing and stressful.

This means that in order to deal effectively with Japanese, particularly those who have not been partially desensitized by long exposure to foreigners, it is very important to treat them with special decorum. The Japanese recognize that most foreigners do not know their etiquette and generally speaking go to what for them is extreme lengths in tolerating Western behavior that they find unpleasant. But they find that the negative effect of putting up with Western behavior is cumulative and that they need some kind of purging mechanism.

There are many areas of business where it is desirable and justifiable to insist that the Japanese change their ways and accept the foreign approach. But one cannot assault their emotions without there being some kind of negative reaction. Learning how to stroke and not provoke a Japanese businessman is part of the process of working with them.

Obviously some of the more conspicuous and damaging things to avoid are appearances of racial or cultural superiority, failure to pay proper respect to Japanese customs and beliefs, and failure to express appreciation or gratitude when it is due. As the Japanese become more self-confident, there may come a time when derogatory remarks about eating raw fish or other traditional Japanese dishes will no longer be regarded as highly insulting and adversely affect business relationships.

Given the power that the traditional culture has on the behavior of the Japanese, it is interesting to note that the culture chains that bind them break easily and quickly once they are outside of the confines of the culture. Within as little as two years outside of Japan, the average Japanese is internationalized to the point that he or she never again fits into the traditional cultural mold, and when these expatriates go home, they face varying kinds and degrees of discrimination because of their un-Japanese attitudes and behavior.

# THE RESENTMENT FACTOR

JAPAN'S ASTOUNDING economic success between the early 1950s and 1970s was viewed by many Japanese as sweet revenge against foreigners who had derided their traditional culture and regarded them as inherently inferior. However, the sudden wealth of Japanese companies and individuals was to add a new twist to the resentment they felt toward the West.

By 1980 there were strong signs that the Japanese business community was feeling beleaguered by the mass of foreigners trying to sell them something or obtain financing for one kind of project or another. What had begun as a trickle in the 1960s had developed into a torrent by the late 1970s. Everybody from presidents, prime ministers, and state governors down to shady hucksters was trying to sell something to the suddenly rich Japanese.

Some of these visitors to Japan came in with a lot of political clout, resulting in promises by the government that did not sit well with the private business sector, exacerbating the feeling that the world was trying to take unfair advantage of Japan.

15

This phenomenon continued until the early 1990s when Japan's financial house of cards collapsed, its seemingly unstoppable growth rate slowed to a crawl, and the supreme confidence of the Japanese in the superiority of their corporate structure and management practices took a stunning blow. The emotional high they had been reveling in suddenly deflated like a pricked balloon.

However, this dash of cold water on the global aspirations and confidence of the Japanese—combined with the economic revival of the U.S. and the emergence of Hong Kong, Taiwan, and South Korea as major competitors—was to have a significantly beneficial effect on their overall mind-set and in their business relations with the rest of the world.

Businessmen, economists, scholars, and a broad range of people across the entire social spectrum began to question the traditional beliefs and practices that had contributed to the economic miracle that had remade Japan and to urge fundamental reforms that would bring Japan closer to the rest of the world in its social and economic systems.

This urging, combined with the continuously evolving world situation, had a major impact on the public as well as the business mind-set of the Japanese, making it a lot easier to do business in Japan. But this does not mean that their attitudes and behavior have changed to the point that they are no longer Japanese in the traditional sense.

The traditional values and traits that have controlled and defined the Japanese for well over a thousand years remain the foundation of the attitudes and behavior of most adult Japanese in their public lives. Understanding and dealing effectively with Japanese businessmen and government officials continue to require in-depth knowledge of a wide range of these enduring cultural factors.

# THE ROLE OF GROUPTHINK

GEORGE ORWELL must have had some familiarity with Confucianism or Japanese culture when he wrote *1984*. One of the Japanese cultural factors that remind me of Orwell's book is called *shudan ishiki* (shuu-dahn ee-she-kee), an old term which means something like "groupthink."

Shudan ishiki remains an important ingredient in the Japanese way of managing, especially in larger companies and despite its now obvious shortcomings. There is a slow but gradual movement in corporate Japan to allow individual thinking and initiative, but it is still in its early stages of development and generally is not pervasive enough to significantly change the way one has to deal with companies.

The groupthink concept that continues to prevail in most Japanese companies makes it imperative that virtually all decisions be made by consensus—a factor that dramatically increases the time it takes to reach decisions. The larger the group involved, the longer it can take for consensus to be achieved.

The obvious advantage of shudan ishiki is that once consensus is reached within a section or department, the wholehearted support and effort of the group helps to ensure that the task has a much better chance of being accomplished efficiently and quickly.

However, there is a downside to the group-think mentality. It is still common for companies, and especially for government agencies, to look at and treat employees as material assets rather than as individuals. Among other things, larger companies and government offices typically switch white collar workers from one section or department to another every two or three years.

The purpose of this rotation system is to provide employees with experience in all of the key sections and departments so they will have a good overview of the entire operation as they move up in rank and responsibility. On the surface, the system has merit, but in any particular section or department it means that a significant percentage of the members are newcomers with little or no knowledge of the work to be done.

The thinking behind this training method, obviously, is that experienced individuals in each of the sections and departments will train and supervise the newcomers and "carry" them until they learn the ropes.

Foreigners dealing with a Japanese company should be cautious about getting stuck with a section member who is new in the group, is not totally familiar with its work, and may have no clout at all.

The custom of transferring personnel from one job to another without regard for the skills involved—and for putting the newest and greenest personnel out in front to handle walk-in visitors or callers—adds to the amount of time and sometimes the confusion involved in contacting and dealing with firms—and is another reason why it is important to have the name of a responsible person in a company before calling or visiting. By immediately giving the name of the individual you wish to contact, you may be able to avoid getting caught up in the mushy outer wall of the Japanese company.

The effects of groupthink go well beyond regarding the company as a single organism made up of virtually identical parts that are interchangeable. It is also responsible for the way the Japanese structure themselves in groups and act together as teams and factions.

And there is, of course, another positive side to the shudan ishiki syndrome. The ingrained ability of the Japanese to work in groups with extraordinary efficiency is one of their primary economic assets. An analogy I like to use is that the Japanese team behaves like a highly trained military squad, while their foreign counterparts tend to behave like a bunch of weekend warriors.

# THE FACTION FACTOR

AN ASPECT of the groupthink syndrome that has a fundamental influence on business in Japan and impacts both directly and indirectly on foreigners dealing with the Japanese is the *habatsu* (hah-bot-sue) or "factions" the Japanese naturally form when they come together.

Historically, Japan's vertically structured feudal society was based on lifelong loyalty to individual leaders from the emperor and shogun on down to the local construction boss. Every political leader and his followers, as well as every business boss and his employees, tended to become a faction, or closely knit group, that acted in unison to achieve goals as well as to defend themselves against competitors or predators. The larger the groups, the more likely there would be multiple factions.

This situation prevailed for centuries, making it more or less second nature for Japanese who come together for any purpose to automatically form factions that quickly take on distinguishable characteristics that determine how one must deal with them to get things done. Sections and departments in Japanese companies tend to act like factions, often making it difficult for them to communicate with each other.

The difference between a Japanese "faction" and a foreign team, company section, or department is not structural. It has to do with the relationship between the individual members, their attitude toward the group, and how the group functions. And this, of course, involves a great many other cultural traits, from the strong sanctions to enforce harmony and the diffusion of personal responsibility to decision by consensus.

Japanese factions vary in size and makeup from a section or a department in a company or government agency to affiliations of companies and politicians. The point is that foreigners dealing with a Japanese company should keep in mind that they are dealing with a closely knit group, not with just the leader or boss or any of the individual members.

This means quick, individually made decisions will not be forthcoming, all members of the group have the right to ask questions and express opinions, and, in principle at least, everyone takes part in all final decisions.

The operation of a section or department in a Japanese company is actually much more democratic than one normally finds in Western companies, which is one of the reasons why it is often difficult for foreigners to understand and accept. In dealing with any Japanese group it helps to take the approach that you are dealing with a small, highly democratic, highly defensive, and often very suspicious, country.

Centuries of conditioning in groupthink and in acting in groups instead of as individuals has resulted in the Japanese developing a highly refined ability to communicate with each other with what one might call "herd telepathy"—but in Japan this phenomenon has far more colorful names, including the "art of the belly."

The strength of the faction system builds upon the groupthink principle in that once a project or course of action is agreed upon—after it has been thoroughly studied and discussed—the whole group works together like a well-trained football team. The weakness of the system is that, again, it is unable to respond quickly, and it tends to pull the caliber of the group well below the level of its most capable members.

# USING THE ART OF THE BELLY

NONVERBAL communication and intuition play a significant role in all personal relations in Japan, including all facets of business. This phenomenon is, of course, a direct outgrowth of a highly sophisticated and stylized culture that is over two thousand years old—a culture in which physical etiquette routinely took precedence over all other considerations. As the centuries passed and the Japanese became more and more homogenized creatures of a monocultural society, packed into a tiny area, living in extended families, and working in consensus-controlled groups, verbal communication became superfluous in many of the common situations of life. To a remarkable degree, everybody thought very much alike, behaved in the same highly controlled manner, and reacted herd-like in virtually all situations.

While this degree of cultural conditioning certainly no longer exists in Japan, enough of it remains in the language, in the common education, and in the common life and work experiences that "communicating without talking" is still ranked high among the characteristic qualities that the Japanese ascribe to themselves.

One area of "Japanese expertise" that plays a key role in business in Japan is known as *haragei* (hah-rah-gay-e) or "the art of the belly." This refers to making decisions on the basis of gut feeling—a visceral reaction to an individual or proposal or situation. Many older Japanese businessmen take great pride in depending on their belly instead of their head in operating their businesses.

What they are using to guide their approach to business is an accumulation of Japanese wisdom that goes back for centuries—their ability to "read" other people, to get their cooperation and help by intuitively knowing how to approach them, treat them, and react to them, and thus meld them into an effective work group.

Many Japanese believe that it is the strength and power that derives from the use of this "Japanese way" that has made their country so successful economically in the world today. Of course, the Japanese art of the belly is generally effective only when the Japanese are dealing with other Japanese—and is the reason why a

Japanese person without extensive international experience feels very uncomfortable in dealing with foreigners. Not being able to "read" foreigners, they cannot anticipate their reactions or be confident in dealing with them.

There is, therefore, a significant amount of constant tension between un-internationalized Japanese and Westerners—tension that disturbs them and tires them.

> For a detailed discourse on the "Japanese art of the belly," see Michihiro Matsumoto's The Unspoken Way—Haragei: Silence in Japanese Business and Society.

One of the many tools foreigners should master in their dealings with Japanese is how to reduce this tension and make their Japanese contacts feel less strained and less tense when they are together—to make their bellies feel good. One of the most important ways of stroking the *hara* (hah-rah) of the Japanese is known as heart-to-heart communication.

# COMMUNICATING
# HEART-TO-HEART

A METHOD of communication in Japan that might be described as more refined or more sophisticated than haragei and that plays an equally important key role in dealing with the Japanese is *ishin denshin* (ee-sheen dane-sheen). This second form of sending and receiving in Japan is often translated as "heart-to-heart communication"—and is what I call "Japanese telepathy."

While haragei refers to visceral feelings, ishin denshin refers to the traditional philosophy and ethics of the Japanese that make "harmony between hearts" the highest priority in relationships. Adhering to the principle of ishin denshin means never saying or doing anything that would upset a business or personal relationship.

This is another aspect of Japan that in the minds of the Japanese separates them from foreigners and is perceived as both an asset and a handicap. They see it as an advantage when they are dealing with other Japanese, and therefore as one of the reasons why Japan is "superior" to other countries. It is of no value to them and becomes a frustration, however, when they are dealing with foreigners because foreigners are not tuned in to the same cultural wavelength.

Japanese businessmen will frequently say it is difficult to deal with foreigners because they cannot communicate heart-to-heart with them and that their goal is to learn English well enough and learn how foreigners do business well enough to establish an ishin denshin relationship with them.

Foreigners, who often do not have sufficient time to learn the Japanese language and Japan's business culture to the extent that they can tap into the telepathic wavelength of their Japanese counterparts, can overcome the handicap to some extent by letting the Japanese know they are aware of the "practice" and have their own version which they are endeavoring to make compatible with the Japanese.

Learning some key Japanese-language words and phrases, a degree of Japanese protocol, and an appreciation of some things Japanese (such as Japanese food and singing in karaoke bars) will go a long way in convincing contacts of your claims about ishin denshin.

It will certainly impress a Japanese businessman if, at a first meeting, you make a point of saying you want to develop a relationship with him that will allow you to communicate heart-to-heart. Interestingly enough, most of the belly-to-belly and heart-to-heart communication that takes place in Japan occurs in the *mizu shobai* (me-zuu show-bye), or "water business," a very insightful euphemism for the night time entertainment trades—something which has also been seen as a particular obstacle for Western women in forming business contacts.

However, a word of advice is in order when it comes to after-hours drinking. It is better to take a page out of the book of many Japanese and not get totally soused during hostess bar outings. On numerous occasions I have been part of Japanese/foreign groups out on the town when one or more of the foreign contingent got sick-drunk and on some occasions passed out, making any form of communication impossible—besides presenting a very negative impression.

Japanese hosts are often relentless in pressing drinks on their foreign guests during hostess bar parties. It is essential that you stay well within your capacity by cutting back sharply after the first few rounds, just sipping the drinks and/or dumping them when nobody is looking, then feigning a degree of drunkenness that keeps you in step with the Japanese side.

If a key Japanese contact leans over and quickly gives you a briefing on the state of your business with him, you want to be able to clearly understand the message and make any appropriate response (even if that is nothing more than nodding your head and thanking him).

The importance of haragei and ishin denshin becomes very clear when you realize that what is not said is often more important than what is said and just as often is the key that opens or locks the door to business.

Learning this form of "Japanese telepathy" is not something one can do quickly or easily. It requires complete immersion in the culture of contemporary Japan, along with a good grasp of the cultural history of the country. This aspect of communication in Japan is one of the primary barriers facing any outsider who attempts to do business with the Japanese and is also why so many foreigners end up having to work through Japanese surrogates to get anything done in Japan.

# MANAGEMENT
# BY INTUITION

GIVEN THE cultural conditioning that results in the Japanese often assigning more importance to feeling than to reasoning, it is not surprising that such things as haragei, or the "art of the belly," and ishin denshin, or "heart-to-heart communication," play a key role in Japanese management. But on the more refined levels of management in Japan one encounters the ultimate in "managing by intuition."

The Japanese word used to express the idea of managing by intuition is *kongen* (kone-gane), which means "root" or "source" in relation to the universe—and may sound like pretty heavy stuff to foreigners who have MBAs instead of MBBs (Masters of Business Buddhism).

Kongen refers to the energy-wisdom that, in Buddhist thought, fuels the universe. According to Buddhist belief, it is accessible to man through meditation, which allows one to tap into the stream of wisdom and energy and make use of it.

Japan's best-known proponent of kongen was the legendary Konosuke Matsushita, founder of the Matsushita empire (National, Panasonic, etc.). Matsushita attributed his extraordinary success to regularly tapping into the intelligence of the universe and decreed that all Matsushita managers would spend a part of their work period tuned in to the universal mind.

While Matsushita was the most prominent modern-day practitioner of managing by intuitive intelligence, it is the key to the management success of all Japanese companies—although I am tempted to label it "Japanese cultural intelligence," since it appears inseparable from the Japanese mind-set and traditional social system.

During the 1950s and early 1960s, many Japanese companies made an attempt to convert their management system to the American paradigm. All of the attempts failed, some of them with tragic results, forcing the companies to go back to the traditional Japanese ways of managing a company. Some of them failed entirely and disappeared.

Many Japanese companies then attempted to follow in Matsushita's footsteps, but what they were doing, regardless of how it was labeled, was following the traditional Japanese way of organizing and treating people and getting an awful lot out of them in the process.

In any event, when the foreigner in Japan runs up against something he thinks doesn't make logical sense, he has probably had an encounter with kongen. If he is inspired to go out and buy himself a cushion to meditate on, he may learn something.

# PASS THE ZEN, PLEASE

I DO NOT advocate that foreigners wanting to do business with the Japanese immediately run to a temple and sign up for a course in Zen Buddhism. But I do suggest that familiarity with the concept and precepts of Zen would be of significant value in dealing with the intangible, esoteric, and philosophical facets of the Japanese business system as well as its facade.

In Japan there is almost always a *tatemae* (tah-tay-my), or facade, and a *honne* (hone-nay)—the reality behind the facade. The universal facade that covers Japan like a blanket is its etiquette system. Other facades include such diverse things as hostess bars in Japan's famous *mizu shobai*: the colorful kimono, which women wear as a "face" to present to the public, is a wonderful facade. Looking at many aspects of Japan, one sees a surface that may hide any number of realities.

The same is true in business. What you see, and what the inexperienced foreigner is apt to take at face value, is often far from the truth. The surface harmony that prevails in most Japanese companies, for example, generally masks a morass of underlying friction and discontent, as wa suffers more and more from the strains of changing lifestyles.

Japanese society in general has traditionally been based on presenting a carefully fashioned image to the public and outside world, taking great pains to camouflage reality behind manners, screens, language, and other opaque barriers. The challenge for the outsider is to discern what is real and what is facade, to see beyond the tatemae to the honne, and one of the skills that has traditionally helped the Japanese see beyond their own illusions is the art of Zen.

The first stage of Zen, for all of its own tatemae, is nothing more than being able to distinguish between what appears to be real (or what we would like to be real) and reality itself. The second stage of Zen requires that one develop the ability to eliminate his own self from the duality of what he is and thinks he is to what exists outside of him and, if he wants to go all the way, merge his being into the one reality.

In the Japanese historical context, Zen was traditionally the vehicle by which people gained extraordinary skill in arts, crafts, and other pursuits. By physical discipline and meditation they first got their own selves under control. Then they learned how to discern the essence of what they saw before them, whether it was a rock, tree, sword, or human being. Then by becoming one with the thing before them, they could use its essence in a natural way.

Probably the most illustrious use of Zen was in the training of swordsmen. After years of rigorous physical and mental training, the greatest swordsmen came close to becoming a part of their swords. Straining the analogy, their swords would therefore strike, perfectly, whatever blow they thought of because they and the sword were the same. The greatest of Japan's sword masters were virtually unbeatable during their peak years. This, of course, represents the Japanese ideal in all things, including business.

The lesson you can take from this facet of the Japanese way is to do your best to separate your emotions and preconceived ideas from any meeting or relationship with a Japanese businessman and attempt to discern the reality behind the visible scenario. This is, of course, just another way of saying determine the facts, the cold, hard facts, before you commit yourself. The idea of taking a Zen-like approach could make it easier, especially with practice.

# PUTTING YOUR BEST FACE FORWARD

IN THE JAPANESE context there is no neat separation between business and personal life. The larger the company, the more apt it is to play a vital role in all the key areas of the lives of its employees—from housing and education to recreation.

Until the late 1990s larger Japanese companies did not hire to fill specific slots; they hired "recruits" (like military draftees) who received general orientation and then were assigned to departments where they received on-the-job training. Those hired as white-collar workers, particularly managerial candidates, were regularly rotated among departments to give them a broad perspective of the company and its operation. Regular employment for men was presumed to be for life.

Domestic and international competition has dramatically changed the way larger companies hire, train, and use their employees. Lifetime employment is no longer guaranteed. People who have worked in other companies and gained valuable skills are now sought after by virtually every major company in Japan—something that was unthinkable until the 1990s. Prior to this, only neophytes right out of high school or university were hired.

Japanese employers traditionally expected total loyalty, total conformity to company policy and culture, and a dedication to work and the welfare of the company that transcended personal concerns.

Given this paternalistic approach to personnel management, Japanese companies gave a high priority to character and personality in their hiring practices. They also gave substantial credence to the ranking of the schools potential employees attended and to their family backgrounds. With some specific exceptions in technical areas, any previous work experience, special knowledge, or aggressive ambition an applicant may have had was generally considered a negative instead of a plus (because these might hinder his being molded into a company man).

The traditional mind-set and practices among older, larger firms have not disappeared from the Japanese scene. But there are cracks in their monolithic policies and practices, as they are being forced to keep up with the times.

Not surprisingly, however, when these Japanese companies are approached by representatives of foreign companies, they tend to use the traditional yardsticks that continue to survive in their own firms to evaluate foreign managers and employees. The evaluation begins with the perceived image of the foreign company—whatever it is—and then jumps immediately to the representatives of that firm—their age, their title, how long they have been with the company, their educational background, any previous relationship with Japan, any personal Japanese contacts they may have, what they know about Japan, what their attitude is toward Japan, how they rank in their own company, why the foreign company chose to approach them (of all the other companies in Japan), who introduced them, and so on ... all personal factors that they want to know before entering into serious discussions with anyone about anything.

The foreigner wanting to do business with the Japanese should anticipate this kind and degree of interest on the personal level and should do everything possible to present the most acceptable image. This means the foreign front man should be selected on the basis of criteria known to be acceptable--and generally speaking, the more impressive the better.

Here is a list of qualifications that are ideal for the foreigner who is going to be assigned to Japan (and are equally applicable to the foreigner visiting Japan in search of a Japanese partner or connection):

1. Since the man (or woman) will have to deal with Japanese managers who are in their late 40s and 50s, or older, he or she should be at least in his or her 30s or 40s.
2. The individual should have a calm, patient personality, be able to think logically and rationally and express himself clearly. If the individual has highly honed intuitive powers, so much the better. He should be secure in his own knowledge and ability and persistent in working toward the company goals.
3. He should have the full confidence and trust of top management back home and have both his responsibilities and authority clearly spelled out. If he does not have decision-making power, he should be guaranteed that when he asks the head office to make a decision, it will be forthcoming in a matter of

hours or days. (Most foreign managers in Japan say they have as much or more trouble getting decisions and action out of their home offices as they do in dealing with the Japanese!)

4. The more experience the individual has already had with Japan and the more he knows about Japan, the better—if he is able to use this experience and knowledge in a nonthreatening, cooperative way that reassures the Japanese rather than turns them off. This includes an outgoing, friendly personality, and—this is very important—liking the Japanese well enough to enjoy their company. It helps if he is a modest drinker and likes a night out on the town (at least once a month). Having a finely honed, but not vulgar, sense of humor is also a major asset.

5. At the same time, the individual should not be naive or gullible, and should at all times insist on the philosophy of fairness and the policy of reciprocity.

6. The individual should have pride in his own country and not bad-mouth it to the Japanese. The Japanese are often critical of the U.S. and other foreign countries, but

they have heard too much criticism by foreigners of their own countries—particularly Americans—and tend to regard such behavior as an attempt to curry favor with them. They may also take it as a sign that the individual is not a person of honor since he will not stand up for his own country.

Japanese often have strong preconceptions of both our weaknesses and strengths, and it does not pay to increase the already stereotypical image they may have of us.

# IDENTIFYING YOUR COMPANY

LARGE FOREIGN COMPANIES going to Japan for the first time often mistakenly assume that their home-country reputation precedes them—that the Japanese know who they are and are impressed. This is often not the case at all. About the only foreign companies whose names are familiar to the Japanese are those who are doing business in Japan and have achieved a high degree of public recognition there. Just like most Westerners, the Japanese tend to ignore things that do not impact directly on their work or personal lives.

The awareness of foreign companies in Japan, including those on the scale of the Fortune 500, naturally tends to be limited to groups that have a professional interest in that particular industry, and even then, with a few exceptions, the awareness is shallow and it is unwise to leave it at this level.

This means that most companies wanting to establish a business relationship with a Japanese firm must take it from the beginning. And while paid-in capital, share of the market, annual sales, profits, and other such numbers are important,

44

the Japanese view is that people make the company. They want to know who the executives are. Before committing themselves to any kind of relationship, they have to get to know, to like, and to trust the foreign executives. They do not go into long-term relationships just on the basis of product and price.

Prior to approaching any Japanese company with any kind of proposal, the foreign firm, regardless of its size, should prepare historical and personal data on its top executives and any lower managers who will be involved with the project. The foreign company must also be prepared to go through a relatively long getting-acquainted period during which personal ties are formed and cemented by various social and cultural means—and the potential Japanese partner checks you out through banks and other connections.

This vital step can be shortened considerably by bringing in third parties that are known to the Japanese side and can, in effect, act as guarantors for the unknown foreign firm. This additional ingredient is even more effective when the third party has a business relationship with the Japanese partner of your choice. There will be more about this later.

Other helpful things when starting from scratch to develop a business relationship with a Japanese company include testimonial letters from political dignitaries (mayors, governors, high-level bureaucrats), scientists and educators with impressive titles and/or achievements, and chief executive officers of large companies whose names at least might be recognizable to the Japanese.

When visited by Japanese representatives of the company you are wooing, you can also get substantial mileage out of arranging for them to meet political dignitaries and have their photos taken with them. The Japanese are also favorably impressed by meetings with well-known authors of business books that have presented Japan in a favorable light, but they are more impressed by movie stars whose films are regularly shown in Japan.

In introducing your company it is unwise to exaggerate or paint a picture that will not stand up under scrutiny and the test of time. The main points to get across are sincerity, integrity, stability, creativity, and goodwill. The Japanese put great stock in all of these attributes, especially creativity. Their home market is so competitive and so conditioned to the regular appearance of new products that they have put creativity at the forefront of their marketing strategy. This ingredient alone is often enough to get their attention.

## KNOWING WHAT YOU ARE TALKING ABOUT

FOREIGNERS who go to Japan cold or make long-distance offers to Japanese companies without having made a serious effort to learn anything about the Japanese market are unlikely to be successful—unless they have a product that is unique and its potential is instantly recognized by the Japanese they approach.

In contrast to this kind of approach, the Japanese are inveterate researchers and collectors of information. Japan's large trading companies have extensive, sophisticated worldwide information gathering networks that are not even approached by foreign commercial companies and are said to surpass the efficiency and effectiveness of such intelligence services as the U.S.'s CIA and the old Soviet Union's KGB.

As early as the beginning of the 1950s the Japanese were swarming the world on research trips. Even small businessmen who wanted to do business abroad or become importers took the time and spent the money to travel overseas, visiting retail outlets, wholesalers, and manufacturers

48

in whatever product area interested them. And what is equally as important, when they found something of interest and took it back to Japan, they generally improved on it.

One such example was a do-it-yourself supply store in Tokyo's Shibuya district based on the American Home Depot or Handyman concept. The display innovations created by the store were startling, and it immediately struck me that American do-it-yourself store operators should come to Tokyo and see what had been done with their idea.

Lack of in-depth knowledge about the Japanese market is probably the biggest failing of most foreign companies wanting to do business in Japan, putting them at a serious disadvantage when they approach a Japanese company. The obvious solution to this problem is that a commitment must be made to spend the necessary money and time to find out what is going on there, how it works, and where they might fit in.

There are a number of options for going about the initial phase of researching an area of the Japanese market. Sources of information include various ministries and agencies of the Japanese government, trade associations, research institutes, marketing

**49**

services, advertising agencies, banks, insurance firms, securities companies, data banks, etc.

A variety of government-issued publications are available on a subscription basis. Some are free. Others can be purchased individually, directly from the publishers or from fulfillment centers. One of the major suppliers of official printed materials on Japan is:

Government Publications Service Center (GPSC)
(Seifu Kankobutsu Sabisu Senta)
1-2 Kasumigaseki, Chiyoda-ku
Tokyo, Japan 100

The GPSC is sales agent for numerous government and private commercial publications on Japan. An annual catalog is available, and mail orders are accepted. Among just Ministry of Finance publications available from the GPSC are the *Annual Report on Business Cycle Indicators, Indicators of Science and Technology, Japanese Economic Indicators, An Outline of Japanese Taxes, Polls on Preferences in National Life, Quality of the Environment in Japan.*

Another source for such publications is Intercontinental Marketing Corporation (IMC),

CPO Box 971, Tokyo, Japan 100-91. IMC is sales agent for most of Japan's English-language publishers. Annual catalogs include *Japan English Books in Print* and *Japan English Magazine Directory.* This directory covers periodicals of all kinds. IMC handles subscriptions and individual sales on a worldwide basis.

A third source for a variety of government and commercial publications on Japan is the Kinokuniya bookstore chain, which has branches in a number of U.S. cities and in several other countries.

Other sources of information on Japan include the commercial departments of foreign embassies in Japan. The data and general information they provide are generally more detailed and more current that other sources. The American Chamber of Commerce in Japan is outstanding in this respect.

American Chamber of Commerce in Japan
Masonic 39 MT Building, 10th floor
2-4-5 Azabudai, Minato-ku, Tokyo 106-0041
Tel (03) 3433-5381
Fax (03) 3433-8454
www.accj.or.jp

Japan Statistical Association
(Nihon Tekei Kyokai)
95 Wakamatsu-cho, Shinjuku-ku
Tokyo, Japan 162

Publications: *Annual Report on the Consumer Price Index*
*Annual Report on the Family Income and Expenditure Survey*
*Annual Report on Labor Force Survey*
*Annual Report on Retail Price Survey*
*Annual Report on Unincorporated Enterprise Survey*
*Employment Status Survey*
*Establishment Census of Japan*
*Family Savings Survey*
*Housing Survey of Japan*
*Japan Statistical Yearbook*

Japan Tariff Association (Nihon Kanzei Kyokai)
Jibiki Building No. 2
4-7-8 Kojimachi, Chiyoda-ku
Tokyo, Japan 102

Publications: *Customs Tariff Schedules of Japan*
*Export Statistical Schedule*

*Import Statistical Schedule*
*Japan Exports and Imports* (commodity by country)
*Japan Exports and Imports* (country by commodity)
*Japan Laws and Regulations Concerning Customs Duties and Customs Procedures*
*Summary Report: Trade of Japan*

Well-informed and well-connected consultants on doing business in Japan are also available in most countries, particularly in the U.S. These include private individuals, consulting firms, law firms, and accounting firms. These sources are generally known to world trade associations, international banking communities, chambers of commerce abroad, and the commercial departments of foreign embassies and consulates in Japan.

Once you have made use of these secondary sources, there is no substitute for going to Japan and doing your own survey, which obviously should include calling on as many places as possible, from commercial attachés at embassies and consulates to chambers of commerce and trade associations (virtually every category of business in Japan has its own trade association listed in the English-language *Japan Yellow Pages*).

53

You should also spend several days visiting retail stores and, if appropriate, factories of interest (most larger factories have visitor programs that can be arranged in advance; some through travel agents such as Japan Travel Bureau, which has hundreds of offices throughout the country).

# COMING UP WITH
# THE RIGHT BAIT

FOREIGNERS who have not done business with Japan before and know very little about the country tend to be naive and simplistic in their opinions about what product or service might succeed in the Japanese market or what kind of overseas investment the Japanese will be interested in.

This attitude ignores a world of reality, beginning with the basics of Japanese thinking and how their business system works, including the highly advanced stage of the Japanese economy with its intense competition. It particularly ignores the comprehensive and intense way the Japanese investigate business opportunities—a process that can take anywhere from months to years. One of the reasons for this is that the cost of failure in Japan is very high.

The foreign company wanting to do business with the Japanese must take an equally long-term view and prepare meticulously for the first encounter. As we have already noted, there are several primary keys to establishing a business relationship with a Japanese company.

**55**

The first key is what you are offering the Japanese. Obviously it has to be something that has merit in their eyes, that fits into their operation and goals and has a high probability of success. The attraction must be strong enough that it will take precedence over anywhere from dozens to hundreds of other projects that are available to the company. It must possess numerous attributes to qualify for serious consideration and have significant potential to win out over other things they could do.

The second key is in the professionalism and thoroughness shown in introducing yourself to potential agents or partners.

Regardless of the product, service, or investment, being able to judge its value or importance to a Japanese company, its suitability for the Japanese market, etc., requires a considerable amount of experience and expertise—or a shot in the dark kind of luck.

The point is rather than take potshots in the dark or keep running things up the flagpole in the hope that serendipity will strike—all of which can be expensive and frustrating and damaging as far as your reputation is concerned—it is better to do some serious homework first. The one thing that stands out in any survey of foreign firms that have succeeded in doing business with the Japanese is that they learned how to use the Japanese system.

The old saying, find a need (or a want) and fill it, applies just as much in Japan as anywhere else. The challenge is to come up with products or investment opportunities that meet this criterion. And unless the Japanese come to you, the best way to do this is for you to go to them—study their psychology, their behavior, their lifestyles, their work habits, their buying habits—or get someone (really good and dependable) to do it for you.

# FOCUSING IN ON
# THE RIGHT CONNECTION

ONCE YOU HAVE determined what product, service, or investment opportunity you are going to offer to the Japanese market, the next challenge is to identify and qualify the most likely prospects for your Japanese connection, whether it is to be an agent, partner, importer, distributor, or investor.

There are numerous factors that must be considered: your company's size and experience, the nature of the product or investment opportunity, the uniqueness factor, any competition, and so on. In the case of products and services to be sold in Japan, the factors having to do with the exclusive group alignment of businesses, the tendency for large Japanese companies to be vertically as well as horizontally integrated, the multilayered nature of the traditional distribution system, the monopolistic tendencies of the large *sogo shosha* (soh-go show-shah) or trading companies, the control exercised by the various ministries over foreign imports (especially the role of the Ministry of Health and Welfare in food imports) are just some of the considerations.

Approaching one of the large trading companies, with their overseas offices and bilingual international staff, may appear to be the obvious and best choice. After all, they are experts in many fields of marketing in Japan; they have extraordinary financial as well as political clout; they have a high image and give a new foreign client instant credibility in the Japanese marketplace; etc.

The downside of going with a large trading company (if they will have you) can be devastating in the long run. Your account becomes one of thousands competing for the attention of qualified managers and often with similar products also handled by the trading company. If your project does not have a high, prime priority, it does not get the best people or the most resources and can easily get stuck in the system.

All of the large trading companies are aligned with specific groups of other companies in banking, manufacturing, distributing, and retailing. Each group has its own "territory" that is vertically structured from top to bottom—from sourcing raw materials to retailing finished products to consumers. In many areas and ways, these groups are exclusive and inclusive and therefore limiting. If you are in the Mitsubishi group, for example, your product may be handled only by other companies affiliated with the same group.

Because of this characteristic Japanese system (which is gradually weakening), there are often occasions when it is better to go with a non-aligned company that can cross "group" borders and will also give a higher priority to your project because it is more important to the firm. A number of recent foreign successes in Japan have been with smaller, unknown entrepreneurial companies founded and operated by exceptionally capable, energetic individuals who overcame all obstacles with the power of their personalities, ideas, and hard work.

The success rate of foreign companies forging alliances with Japanese companies is relatively low, however, and should serve as a warning to companies contemplating doing business in Japan. The reasons for the low batting average are invariably the same. The foreign company took the fast, easy way out and signed up without really knowing what they were getting into.

It is, in fact, very difficult for a foreign company not intimately familiar with Japan to make a sound decision about a potential Japanese connection.

There are so many factors and variables, many of them subtle and invisible, that should be taken into consideration. While it is possible to find out a great deal about a company, both its strengths and its weaknesses, in just a few days of investigation, it is still difficult for a foreign company without extensive Japan experience to make the best choice for a long-term relationship.

There is a tendency for foreigners to accept what they see and hear in Japan at face value, often to their later chagrin. Reality in Japan is often not what the foreigner perceives it to be.

Both Japanese and foreigners often make decisions on the basis of "belly feelings." As stated previously, this is a significant aspect of the Japanese way of doing business, but problems arise when these decisions are crosscultural. The gut feeling a foreigner gets from a Japanese situation is much more likely to be wrong than right. It is generally much safer to go with the professional advice of a third party than depend on feelings.

Often the most practical recourse open to the foreign company, regardless of its size, is to enlist the aid of third parties in Japan—bankers, accountants, government officials, advertising agencies, market research firms, consultants, and lawyers as well as people in the business category concerned—to advise them.

Of course, there are exceptions, such as when you are dealing with an entrepreneurial type whose character and personality tip the odds in his favor or with the founder-owner of a so-called "one-man company" who calls all of the shots, and makes a strong personal commitment to you and your project. However, in general, finding the right connection is invaluable.

# FINDING THE
# RIGHT CONNECTION

FINDING AND MAKING connec-
tions in Japan may not be as difficult as it first
appears, even for novice newcomers. As already
mentioned, obvious contact points include
Japanese embassies and consulates abroad. Their
information is invariably dated, but they can provide names and addresses of other more current
sources of information. The commerce departments or ministries (and regional field offices) of
respective countries are also sources for general
information on doing business in Japan, including very pertinent data on the laws, regulations,
and procedures for importing and exporting.

The next obvious contact points are the appropriate embassies and consulates maintained by foreign countries in Japan. The Tokyo embassies of all
the leading nations have very active commercial
sections dedicated to helping their businesses succeed in Japan. The larger embassies, in particular
the American, British, German, French, Canadian,
and Australian embassies, are especially active in
the commercial area, providing numerous business
services to their nationals.

The American Embassy in Tokyo operates a Business Information Center that offers various services to U.S. businessmen, from advice on whom to contact and helping set up appointments to assistance in negotiating with private companies as well as government agencies. The *Japan Market Information Report,* published by the center, can be very valuable for keeping up with what is going on in the Japanese market. The center also maintains a large library of information about Japanese companies.

Next in line and closer still to the action are the foreign chambers of commerce in Tokyo. The American Chamber of Commerce in Japan (ACCJ) is one of the most active, with several ongoing research and service committees designed to provide members with up-to-date information about every important aspect of doing business in Japan, from market research, advertising, distribution, and marketing to taxes, housing, and schools for expatriate kids.

The ACCJ conducts regular "business breakfasts" for its members and guests, featuring speakers and panelists who are experts in various aspects of Japan's business world.

Any businessman can join the American Chamber of Commerce in Japan (membership is not limited to Americans). There is a nonresident membership for businesspeople who live abroad and want the advantage of receiving the chambers various publications and reports and utilizing its office on visits to Japan. Becoming a member of the chamber plugs you into one of the largest and most effective foreign-oriented networks in the country.

Other prime contact points are the various service clubs that are active and popular in Japan. Probably the two largest and most important are the Rotary Club and the Kiwanis Club. The Japanese take membership in these clubs very seriously and also look at them as contact points for their own international relations. Foreign members of these clubs can invariably tap into the Japanese membership and take advantage of a wide network of contacts. See the *Japan Yellow Pages* for current numbers and addresses.

Sister-city relationships are another good contact point for beginning to establish a Japanese network. Some of the more aggressive cities around the world have sister-city relations with as many as a dozen Japanese cities, from Kagoshima at the southern tip of Kyushu to Sapporo on the northern island of Hokkaido.

Professional associations are another avenue for getting inside the outer moat of Japan. There is an association for virtually every endeavor, cultural, social, educational, scientific, economic, etc. Visits to the appropriate office will usually provide you with a list of potential contacts.

On the business side, foreign as well as Japanese banks are key contact points and are often all you need to get started. The foreign branches of Japanese banks can be especially helpful, as can the branches of foreign banks in Japan. The larger Japanese trading companies have offices all over the world and can often provide points of entry into the Japanese business community.

There are a number of annual English-language directories that provide the names and addresses of all the entities mentioned above, plus hundreds more, which are available in hotel bookshops in Japan as well as in many outlets abroad that specialize in books on Japan.

These publications include the *Japan Yellow Pages* and directories of the foreign subsidiaries and branches of Japanese companies around the world, including the *Directory of Offices and Affiliates of Japanese Companies* in the U.S. and Canada. There are also *Japan Yellow Pages* published in Los Angeles and in New York covering those areas and available in Kinokuniya and other Japan-related book outlets.

# PUTTING YOUR LIFE
# ON THE LINE

ONE OF THE AREAS in which the Japanese most often find fault with foreign companies interested in doing business in Japan is commitment. They point out repeatedly, and rightly so, that anyone who wants to succeed in Japan—whether Japanese or foreign—must make a firm long-term commitment. Many foreign companies that have come into Japan have given up before getting started or withdrawn at the first serious setback.

There are a dozen or more aspects to the Japanese rationale. First, it simply takes longer to get things started in Japan than it does in such freewheeling economies as the U.S. and Canada. The reasons for this slow pace range from the cold molasses speed of the bureaucracy to the need for establishing supporting networks of personal relationships over a period of time. Another reason is that business itself is done in a much more personal way, requiring a much larger time investment to make and maintain contacts.

Business relationships are not based solely on products and profits. Even more important are the confidence, trust, and loyalty that are the hallmark of the Japanese system—things that require years and a lot of investment to develop.

The Japanese are acutely aware that their business system is extremely difficult for foreigners to master and that the Japanese cultural environment in general constitutes a major obstacle to a foreign company coming in and succeeding in Japan. They agree, on the one hand, that the system itself is at fault and should be changed, but on the other hand, they note that they also have to operate within the system and, if they can do it, foreigners who really try should also be able to.

As the Japanese have become more successful and self-assertive, they have become more critical of both the commitment and the ability of foreign companies wanting to penetrate the Japanese market. This does not make it easier for the foreign company, since there is a degree of built-in prejudice from the beginning and a tendency for the Japanese to maintain the present system because it works well for them and acts as a barrier to keep foreign companies at bay.

The official Japanese stance of favoring the entry of more foreign companies into Japan can be a key to making it happen, once the foreigner has shown the necessary commitment. The foreigner, as one of his first moves, should systematically solicit the cooperation and support of as many Japanese government offices and agencies as possible, openly and frankly asking for their help. Your early contacts, including the commercial department of your embassy in Tokyo, can advise you on the government entities whose advice and endorsement would benefit you.

# AVOIDING THE
# SECOND-CLASS PITFALL

THE JAPANESE obsession with quality has a broad impact that influences all areas and levels of life and work in the country. The Japanese image of most foreign products as being inferior to their own—whether the image is right or wrong—is well recognized as a major problem for its foreign trading partners. This facet of Japanese culture is of immediate concern to the foreign company wanting to do business with Japan for the first time because it may prevent the company from even getting onto the playing field.

The first impression the Japanese get of a foreign company is often its stationery, brochures, annual reports, and maybe catalogs. The impression imparted by these printed materials goes a long way toward setting the company's image in their minds. If the materials are not well designed and well printed on attractive paper stock, the image is negative and immediately gives the impression that the company is not professional, not sophisticated, not successful, and not concerned about its image.

Foreign companies approaching Japan often begin with two strikes against them because they go in with second- or third-class printed materials—because they are less concerned about the quality of the materials and see no reason for spending the kind of money necessary to get first-class or superior design and printing. Besides doing without professional design, too many foreign companies also stint on printing by going to small neighborhood quick-print shops for their work.

Unless the foreign company is large and well-known in Japan (in which case it may be able to successfully flout local standards), it is strongly advised that all materials to be used in any presentation or promotion be especially designed and printed with Japanese quality standards in mind. As it happens, the Japanese are especially sensitive to design and printing and automatically make comparisons between Japanese printing and foreign printing. Not surprisingly, they believe their printing and design industries are the best in the world.

Going in with lower quality printing reinforces the Japanese belief that foreigners are basically not concerned about quality, and this reflects badly on foreign companies in other areas as well.

# GOING IN ALONE

MORE AND MORE foreign companies entering Japan are sidestepping the problems of finding, qualifying, and allying with Japanese agents or partners by going in on their own, making their own distribution contacts or establishing their own systems. While this approach presents a different set of factors, it obviously works for some kinds of operations.

Probably the biggest factor in whether or not a foreign company decides to go it alone in Japan is a strong desire to avoid the hidebound multileveled distribution system, with its age-old loyalties and stranglehold on both manufacturers and retailers. Other obvious factors are maintaining more control over their operation and reaping more of the rewards, including the value that comes from learning how to market in Japan directly.

As the consumer economy has matured and the number and variety of new retail chain stores without long ties to wholesalers have mushroomed, it has offered more opportunities for direct distribution by both Japanese and foreign companies. Direct-mail marketing had also become a major industry in Japan by the 1980s and is growing at an impressive annual rate.

The key for successful direct distribution to the retail trade as well as direct-marketing to consumers in Japan is invariably in hiring highly qualified Japanese managers and, again, persistence over a long period of time to develop the necessary relationships, awareness, and trust. The Japanese touch is usually essential in being able to deal effectively with all of the players, since language along with all the other nuances of the Japanese way of doing things is generally too much of a barrier for foreign managers to overcome on their own.

This means that a great deal of your initial effort must be in identifying exceptionally qualified people and then making them an offer they cannot refuse. Several management recruiting agencies in Tokyo specialize in this area and are well-known to the local foreign chambers of commerce and the commercial departments of foreign embassies.

# FIGHTING SPIRIT

NOT SURPRISINGLY, the Japanese have a special word to describe the qualities that are ideal in a businessman, especially one who is to be entrusted to launch a new project or new product. This term, *konjo* (kone-joe), means "nature" or "spirit," and in this context means "fighting spirit."

The origin of the konjo concept no doubt goes back to the days (actually not so long ago) of the samurai, Japan's feudalistic warrior class, whose training included not only mastering an array of martial arts but also mastering and steeling the spirit to the point that they could slit open their own bellies in a formalized suicide ritual when the occasion called for it.

It is still common in Japan to think of business strategy and tactics in military terms (the books of Chinese and Japanese military strategists have long been required reading for those aspiring to careers in management). A *konjo ga aru otoko* (kone-joe gah ah-rue oh-toe-koe) or "man with fighting spirit" type of manager who will go after his goals with all the dedicated planning and ferocity of a warrior who is going to attack a well-entrenched enemy, knowing there will be no quarter given and no retreat, remains the standard by which all others are measured.

The foreign company looking for a representative or a top employee in Japan, especially one that is to head up a marketing operation, would be well advised to add konjo to the list of qualifications for such an individual. Just using the term to your contacts and any recruiters you might engage will immediately clarify what kind of person you are looking for and the way you intend to approach the market

# RULES OF EMPLOYMENT

IF YOU ARE contemplating establishing your own company in Japan, it is essential to keep in mind that labor laws in Japan are comprehensive and precise. It is critical that foreign companies setting up an operation in Japan obtain local expert assistance in providing not only the right legal framework for their operations but also an effective cultural environment for their employees.

There is a strong tendency for foreigners to inject some of the laws and customs of their own country into their rules of employment for their Japanese staff. This almost never works well, except perhaps in an office with only two or three people, and each time an additional member is added to the staff the more likely it is that it will not work at all.

As much as they might like the sound of the American or European way of management, and as often as they might say they prefer it and want it when being considered for employment by a foreign firm, un-internationalized Japanese invariably find that it does not suit either their emotional needs or their concept of what is fair.

Foreign companies that are persuaded by the initial reaction of Japanese employees, or insist on their own on utilizing Western management practices, almost always find themselves in trouble within a short period of time. There have been numerous cases where the problems were so deep and fundamental there was no practical way out, and the companies went under.

Once the Japanese-style *shumu kisoku* (shuu-muu kee-soe-kuu), or work rules, are in place—and signed by every Japanese employee—you can add some personal or Western flavor to your management style if you find it effective, but the protection of having precedent-and-court approved work rules is essential.

# GOING IN WITH A
# JAPANESE CONNECTION

IF YOU OPT to go into Japan through a Japanese connection, your primary challenge will be to develop and maintain a working relationship with the Japanese side that is close enough and effective enough to protect your interests and allow you to make a contribution to the project. This is not as easy as it might first appear. Because of the nature of the business environment and the Japanese way of doing things, you have often put the future of the project in Japanese hands.

As soon as the agreement is signed, chances are both your goals and the way to achieve them will begin to diverge. The Japanese side will naturally take the position that they know more about how to do things in Japan than you do and will often proceed without explaining or informing you of their moves. No matter how strong your position is on paper, the Japanese side will usually be the one that implements the project and sets its tenor and tone.

It is therefore very important that you come to a full, long-range understanding of mutual goals prior to signing any agreement and that checks and balances that empower you to influence the broad scope of the program be written into the agreement.

As always, it is essential to have your own man in Japan—Japanese or foreign—who has the experience and knowledge to effectively interface between you and the Japanese side and whom you can trust completely.

Whether in joint ventures or wholly owned foreign companies, there is invariably a natural division between the foreign staff and the Japanese staff, and there is often competition for influence among the Japanese staff factions, which, whether intended or not, tends to isolate the foreign personnel.

In wholly owned foreign firms in Japan that have foreign CEOs, there is a strong tendency for the Japanese side to assume that eventually the foreign CEO will be replaced by a Japanese CEO. The rationale is that, after all, the company is in Japan so a Japanese CEO can naturally do a better job than a foreign CEO—and this remains true despite the success stories of some high-profile foreign CEOs in Japan . . . whose numbers remain minuscule.

80

The built-in belief that the CEO should be Japanese tends to set up a great deal of competitive tension within companies, often with one or more of the more powerful Japanese managers constantly maneuvering to enhance their positions and to isolate the foreign CEOs.

Of course, the upside of going in with a Japanese connection is that the Japanese side does know how to operate in Japan, does have connections, and, if sincere, aggressive, and capable, can make a significant contribution to the success of the project. By the same token, the foreign company going through a Japanese connection virtually forfeits the opportunity to learn the Japanese market and how to do business there on its own.

# THE IMPORTANCE OF
# GOING TO JAPAN

THE JAPANESE knew in the 1950s
and '60s that the ultimate key to learning about
foreign markets and doing business abroad was to
travel overseas to actually see the markets and
experience dealing with their foreign counterparts
on their home ground. This is a lesson that those
wanting to do business with Japan must also learn.

Reading books and listening to others talk
about working with the Japanese are a good
beginning that can save a lot of time, expense, and
frustration, but not going any further is like reading a romance novel without ever being in love or
a guide to riding a bicycle and never actually getting on one. It is a one-dimensional exercise that
is far from the real thing.

To really grasp how the Japanese do business
and how to deal with them effectively you have
to take your clothes off and jump into the water;
you have to feel and taste the nuances of their
attitudes and behavior; you have to physically
absorb the system into your body.

To do this even to a minor degree, you must go
to Japan and personally experience it, physically

82

and emotionally as well as intellectually. This means that once you are in Japan you have to get out of the international hotels and office buildings and spend time in department stores, on shopping streets, in restaurants, and in hostess bars, in major transportation terminals, on trains and in subways, in schools, and if you can arrange it, in the homes of ordinary people.

This is the kind of investment of time and money that the average foreigner is all too often reluctant to make and is one of the reasons why more foreign companies are not in the Japanese market. Ultimately, it could be one of the reasons why foreign businesses lose out in their own home markets to Japanese companies that are more aggressive, more determined, and work harder.

Ideally, the foreign company wanting to do business in Japan should do what the Japanese do when they want to penetrate a foreign market—send one or more of their best people there, for as much as a year or more, to do nothing but study the country, the people, the language, the market, and how the business system works, including cultural insights and skills that will help them live and work in the society.

# GREASING THE SKIDS

REGARDLESS of the kind of project or the nature of the business in which one proposes to become involved with an individual Japanese or a Japanese company, one of the key elements in establishing a relationship is to go in with a *shokaijo* (show-kie-joe), or "introduction," from someone or some company of sufficient stature to get you across the moat, through the gates, and into the presence of a top executive.

Being group-oriented with extraordinarily heavy obligations to their families, relatives, school friends, employers, and the government, the Japanese have traditionally avoided casual contact with strangers that might develop into more obligations, competition, or conflicts of interest with outside groups. Also being conditioned to avoid individual responsibility, the Japanese have always been reluctant to take any kind of personal initiative on behalf of someone they do not know.

Traditional protocol made it mandatory that the only acceptable way the Japanese could develop a new relationship was if the person concerned was introduced to them by a mutual friend or third party with whom they had an established, positive relationship—and who would, in theory at least, take responsibility for the behavior of the person being introduced.

In the 1950s and '60s foreign businesses often ignored this protocol in their activities in Japan, either out of ignorance or arrogance. Foreigners regularly went to Japanese companies without appointments and were almost always welcomed courteously, often by the highest ranking individual in the office or company at that time. This special catering to foreigners diminished significantly in the 1970s and is now rare, if it exists at all, especially in larger firms.

While the historical sanctions enforcing shokaijo protocol have weakened considerably, it is still an expected and important facet of Japanese behavior. Generally speaking, Japanese companies will not respond to any approach made by people or companies they do not know, unless the approach is through an acceptable introduction. Self-introductions by phone or letter, which are perfectly acceptable in many Western countries, usually do not work as well, or at all, in Japan.

Acceptable introductions on a personal level include ones from a friend or relative, a former professor, or a benefactor. On a company level, acceptable introductions to specific individuals include personal connections as well as established business connections, such as managers or executives of banks, other companies, associations, and government agencies.

The power or effectiveness of an introduction is, of course, determined by a number of factors. On a company level, an introduction from the department head of Mitsui Trading Company or the Bank of Tokyo is obviously going to carry more weight than one from a small, relatively unimportant enterprise. Likewise, an introduction from a well-known professor of a high-ranking university—to a former student—can gain you quick access to an otherwise unapproachable person.

When a Japanese wants to meet someone new, on a personal or business level, the first thing he does is review his list of contacts to see if he knows anyone who has a relationship with the individual or company he wants to call on and can provide him with an introduction. In earlier years, such introductions almost always involved physically taking the mutual contact's business card to the meeting and presenting it to the third party. Nowadays, it is usually sufficient to just make verbal reference to the go between, generally by phone when calling in to set up an appointment, or by e-mail.

Foreigners in Japan are no longer automatically excused from following established custom and in this case are strongly advised to take advantage of the customary etiquette for very practical reasons—it means the drawbridge will be let down, and you will be able to cross the outer moat surrounding the company and state your case as an honorary insider instead of yelling across the ramparts as a stranger.

As part of your research to identify the company you want to approach and the individuals within the company that would be the most appropriate for you to talk to, you should also identify people who can provide you with introductions—preferably business contacts that are important to them, but personal contacts are also acceptable as a second choice.

The ideal situation is to have an introduction to someone on the director level and then, through him, to move down to the department head level and from there to the appropriate section or sections where the work you are interested in actually takes place.

# GETTING HELP FROM EXPERTS

CULTURAL ARROGANCE and lack of cross-cultural experience often result in foreigners automatically presuming that they can establish themselves in Japan without any outside help. Most cannot, and many of those who do eventually succeed could have saved themselves a lot of time, frustration, and investment by enlisting the aid of *sodanyaku* (soe-dahn-yah-kuu), "consultants," or *chukai-sha* (chuu-kie-shah), "go-betweens," whose specialty is bridging the foreign-Japanese cultural and communications gaps.

The personal nature of business in Japan, the role of long-term connections in getting in to see the right people and getting things done, the subtle nuances of business relationships, the list of dos and don'ts, and the experience necessary to maneuver one's way through the protocol and maze of the Japanese system are not something that one picks up overnight.

Conventional wisdom, as learned by expatriates who have been stationed in Japan for a long time, is that it takes a minimum of three years of on-the-job experience to become fairly efficient in operating with and within the Japanese system.

Most foreign companies setting up operations in Japan depend on their new Japanese employees to act as their advisors, go-betweens, and buffers in dealing with the Japanese bureaucracy and marketplace. Some are fortunate enough to find and employ very capable Japanese people who can bridge the gap for them. This kind of serendipity is rare, however, and companies that are not so fortunate generally have a difficult and expensive time.

Foreign companies seeking to establish relationships and deal with Japanese companies from abroad may face fewer problems directly, but if they do not have in-house expertise (that is genuine), their chances of consummating a relationship which they themselves initiated with a Japanese company are minimal.

The recommended solution is an obvious one that is all too often ignored—obtaining the services of an experienced consultant and/or go-between. I distinguish between the two because the sodanyaku or consultant is often involved only on the sidelines, giving advice and helping to develop strategy and tactics, while the chukai-sha or go-between gets down into the trenches, meets the other side face-to-face, and represents the interest of his or her client. Most go-betweens are usually qualified to act as consultants as well, but many consultants are not qualified to be go-betweens.

There are several classes and levels of consultants, starting with Westerners whose primary credentials are academic—they've read a lot of books and maybe done some fieldwork—and then those who have lived and worked in Japan. A few of the latter speak Japanese well enough to conduct business in the language. There are also foreign consultants of Japanese ancestry who have firsthand experience and are fluent in the language as well as native Japanese consultants who are well versed in English and primarily service foreign clients.

Because of the sensitive nature of dealing with Japanese companies and the extraordinary amount of knowledge and experience necessary for doing it effectively, most of the best chukai-sha are Japanese who have become at least semi-bilingual and bicultural and are able to function in both environments.

There are only a limited number of non-Japanese offering their services as consultants on doing business with the Japanese who are in fact qualified to serve as go-betweens as well and perform both functions. A significant percentage of these are of Japanese ancestry. As a general guideline, any go-between, Japanese or non-Japanese, should have spent at least ten years in Japan working in and/or with Japanese companies on a daily basis with a broad scope of experience.

It should be emphasized that virtually all problems that arise between Japanese and foreign companies begin and end with communication failures, not only in the sense of language but in cultural communication as well. It is therefore essential that any go-between you might retain should be thoroughly experienced in all aspects of the language and the business culture.

In considering the use of go-betweens, the higher the professional standing of the individuals the better. The ideal chukai-sha is a successful ex-businessman or high government official, at least in his late 40s—and often the older the better (since he will be dealing with men in this age level and above)—whose background and connections are impressive enough that he is automatically afforded a high degree of respect.

Probably the best sources for lists of recommended consultants and go-betweens are the various foreign chambers of commerce in Japan.

# BORROWING FACE FROM ADVISORS

ANOTHER tried and proven technique for success in dealing with the Japanese for any purpose on any level is making use of "advisors." In fact, this is a practice that goes way beyond surface indications. It is an institution sanctified by the ages and incorporates the Japanese philosophy of venerating and taking care of the elderly—with very practical applications.

When high-level company executives or government bureaucrats retire, it is common for them to be appointed advisors to their former organizations, usually for life. It is also common for them to become advisors to other companies or organizations. This means they will continue to have income. It also means that the connections and experience they accumulated over a lifetime continue to be used and the "face" they have in their industry does not go to waste.

Virtually every Japanese organization, including those of very modest size, has its advisors. Larger companies and organizations also retain professors and scientists who are still active in their fields along with those who have retired.

One of the first things the Japanese are likely to do in setting up a new enterprise is to add a list of advisors to their roster. Many government and cultural organizations will have from three or four to twenty or more advisors.

In academic and cultural circles especially, but in some political and commercial operations as well, these lists of advisors are often just window dressing, added to give legitimacy and image to the organization. In such cases, the advisors are seldom called on to give any advice, but they are invited to receptions and other events where their presence is an asset. Of course, they are paid fees for lending their names to such enterprises.

The benefit that a well-known advisor can bring to a company in Japan should not be underestimated, however, even when he actually gives little or no advice. In these cases it is his "face" that is being used. But there are just as many advisors who do in fact play active roles in the companies that retain them, not only giving advice but also opening doors and making connections.

The foreign company wanting to do business with Japan, whether in Japan or abroad, will invariably find that a highly respected advisor (or advisors) can make the road much smoother and shorter. I recommend that any company contemplating going into Japan put finding a suitable advisor (or more) on the top of their list of things to do.

Companies already in Japan that do not have advisors, and believe they could or should be doing better, might be able to make a breakthrough with the help of one or more high-profile individuals in their area of business. Ex-bureaucrats and professors are the most popular advisors.

# INVITING THE JAPANESE TO VISIT YOU

**I**F YOU ARE the one that makes the first contact with Japanese firms, and subsequently visit them in Japan as part of your presentation, it is good psychology and often good business to invite them to visit you in your office for a continuation of the dialogue or negotiations. The more important the project and the more interested the Japanese side, obviously the more likely they are to accept the invitation.

I make a point of this here because smaller foreign companies often fail to take advantage of getting the Japanese to come to them on their home ground; oftentimes because they are small and are afraid the Japanese side would not be sufficiently impressed. This is usually not a good excuse, because your size and everything else about you is most likely going to come out anyway, especially if you are the one that approached the Japanese company, since they are usually very meticulous in checking out potential suppliers or partners.

If you can get the Japanese to come to you, you have a number of home-ground advantages.

They will automatically fall into the "dealing with foreigners outside of Japan mode," meaning you can follow your own native protocol in dealing with them in your overall approach and just cater to their *Japaneseness* on the personal side, such as taking them to a good Japanese or Chinese restaurant if they have been outside of Japan for several days (by which time they will appreciate a familiar meal) and giving them a gift when they leave.

It also obviously gives you an opportunity to thoroughly acquaint them with your operation from the ground up, significantly reducing the amount of time it would normally take to establish the relationship you want with them. Of course, if they are not impressed enough with your company to continue pursuing the project, that is another matter. In any event, being frank and forthright in representing yourself and your company is the best policy. Companies that misrepresent themselves to the Japanese invariably get caught.

Larger Japanese companies that are interested in the products or services of a small foreign company will not normally expect the small firm to pick up the tab for their travel or hotel accommodations if you invite them to visit you.

It is good etiquette, however, to pay all restaurant bills when you dine with them except when the visitors make a point of inviting you out, usually on their last night in town. In their own country the Japanese themselves are exceptionally generous about paying restaurant and other miscellaneous expenses of foreign guests, often saying things like "You are in Japan. You are our guest."

Interestingly, the Japanese generally do not expect the same degree of generosity from foreigners whom they visit abroad. The apparent reason for this attitude is that the Japanese have traditionally had a reputation of being big spenders when it came to entertaining and taking care of guests. In earlier times this was partly to demonstrate a cavalier attitude toward material wealth and partly to demonstrate their superiority. On the other hand, to accept such generosity from an outsider, especially a foreigner, would lower their ego and put them in an inferior position.

Many foreigners coming to Japan have an image of the Japanese as being rich and generous, and the more parsimonious of them will deliberately hold back in restaurants and other places until the Japanese pick up the bills.

Usually, foreign visitors don't have to go to such extremes to avoid paying a bill.

The Japanese generally regard themselves as the host unless they are specifically invited out. I have often seen and been involved in outright struggles with Japanese over food and bar bills. But there is a time to give in and a time to pay your own way. Sometimes, in order to pay your own way as well as the way of your Japanese counterparts you must slip away from the table early and pay the bill before the meal or party ends—or give advance instructions that the bill be surreptitiously delivered to you.

There is the strong feeling among the Japanese that if they pay such bills they have demonstrated their sincerity, generosity, kindness, goodwill, and various other "Japanese" attributes of which they are especially proud—which is alright up to a point.

My point is that foreign businesspeople should set a limit on the amount and volume of hospitality they will accept from the Japanese side. Otherwise their reputations will suffer, and they will lose face in the eyes of their Japanese contacts.

# THE STRUCTURE OF A
# JAPANESE COMPANY

THE ORGANIZATION or structure of Japanese companies is simple enough and is similar enough to Western companies that it can be misleading, with those who are unfamiliar with the inner workings of Japanese companies presuming they also function very much like foreign firms.

Companies are normally divided into *bu* (buu), or departments, and *ka* (kah), or sections. Each department is made up of a number of sections. There are the usual departments divided by function and ranging from advertising to sales. Sections within departments are also divided by function and are the key working units in all companies.

Each bu (department) is headed by a *bucho* (buu-choe), or department head, who usually goes by the English title of general manager and is the equivalent of a vice president in American companies. His assistant, the *bucho dairi* (buu-choe die-ree), is the deputy general manager.

Each ka (section) is headed by a manager called a *kacho* (kah-choe), who may have one or two assistants called *kakaricho* (kah-kah-ree-choe), or supervisors. Each section is made up of a team of six or eight to sixteen or more people who all do basically the same kind of work. Teams consist of men and women ranging from the youngest recruits right out of school up to the kacho, who is usually a veteran of at least fourteen years. It usually takes around eight years to reach the level of kakaricho.

Desks in the ka are usually arranged in an elongated box fashion with the kacho at the head and the supervisors to his right or left. The lowest ranking member of the team is normally at the foot of the box. As team members pile up seniority, they gradually work their way up the line of desks.

The ka making up a department are arranged more or less classroom style, with the department chief at the head of the room—usually farthest from the door and often with his back to a window. The more important the section, the more centrally located it may be in relation to the desk of the department head.

The one Japanese department that few if any foreign companies have is the *Somu Bu* (Soe-muu Buu), or General Affairs Department. This is the catchall department. It handles company mail, maintains the company files and stock ledgers, coordinates interdepartmental relations, handles public relations, and steers visitors to the right section. The first contact with most large Japanese companies is with the Somu Bu.

Since it is the ka that produces the work in Japanese companies, the kacho in all of the sections and departments that have anything to do with a project are the key people with whom the outsider must interface. Just talking to the higher executives and bucho is generally not enough.

It is always advisable and often essential that one meet and cultivate a close relationship with several kacho in a company with which you are doing business or want to do business. Other typical departments in Japanese companies are the:

Accounting Department—*Keiri Bu* (Kay-e-ree Buu)

Advertising Department—*Koho Bu* (Koe-hoe Buu)

International Department—*Kokusai Bu* (Koe-sie Buu)

Personnel Department—*Inji Bu* (Jeen-jee Buu)

Planning Department—*Kikaku Bu* (Kee-kah-kuu Buu)

Production Department—*Seizo Bu* (Say-e-zoe Buu)

Public Relations Department—*Shogai Bu* (Show-guy Buu)

Purchasing Department—*Shizai Bu* (She-zie Buu)

Sales Department—*Eigyo Bu* (A-ee-g'yoe Buu)

Larger Japanese companies have three levels of employees: the *yakuin* (yah-kuu-een), or the executives from director on up; the *bukacho* (buu-kah-choe), or middle and lower managers, made up of the section and department heads and their assistants; and the *hira-shain* (hee-rah-shah-een), or "level" employees, who have no rank. The table of organization in a large company looks like this:

# The Structure of a Japanese Company

Stockholders
*Kabunushi* (Kah-buu-nuu-she)

Board of Directors
*Torishimari Yakkai*
(Toe-ree-she-mah-ree yahck-kie)

Chairman of the Board
*Kaicho* (Kie-choe)

Representative Director
*Daihyo Torishimari Yaku*
(Die-h'yoe Toe-ree-shee-mah-ree Yah-kuu)

President
*Shacho* (Shah-choe)

Director and Executive Vice President
*Senmu Torishimari Yaku*
(Sen-muu Toe-ree-she-mah-ree Yah-kuu)

Director and Senior Vice President
*Jomu Torishimari Yaku*
(Joe-muu Toe-ree-she-mah-ree Yah-kuu)

103

Standing Auditor
*Jonin Kansayaku* (Joe-neen Kahn-sah-yah-kuu)

Department Head
*Bucho* (Buu Choe)

Section Head
*Kacho* (Kah-choe)

Supervisor
*Kakaricho* (Kah-kah-ree-choe)

Unranked employees
*Hira-shain* (Hee-rah Shah-een)

A representative director (daihyo torishimari yaku) has power of attorney to act in the name of the company, and larger firms may have more than one. In some companies, ranking bucho may also be directors. Generally, all of the directors of Japanese companies are in-house directors—something that is slowly changing among the more international firms.

In addition to regular department heads (bucho) some companies have *senmon bucho* (sen-moan buu-choe), or "specialty chiefs," who are given the title because of their special skills, but have no department under them.

A primary difference between Japanese companies and most Western companies is that top executives in larger Japanese firms, regardless of their title, do not have the degree of executive power that is common in the United States. Many of them, in fact, do little or no "managing" in the usual Western meaning of the term, which connotes going around and giving orders to people.

Top Japanese executives set the general policies of their companies, but planning and day-to-day management are in the hands of middle and lower management who use a consensus approach to decision-making.

In most large Japanese companies managers don't tell anybody what to do. New employees assigned to ka are given orientation, but as for actual work, they are expected to learn by watching and asking coworkers who are more advanced and by doing.

Some presidents of Japanese companies spend a lot of time involved with the training and nurturing of future managers in the company, frequently taking part in company interviews and orientations. One of the primary obligations of many bucho is to identify especially capable people in their departments and help groom them for higher management positions.

Foreigners proposing to do business with the Japanese should keep in mind that impressing the chairman of the board, the president, or other high-level executives is a nice thing to do but that in all likelihood it will be the kacho and bucho who determine whether or not their projects will fly, based on their research, evaluation, recommendations, and actions.

Again, the ideal situation is to have an introduction to a top-level executive and after the formalities make sure you are introduced to the bucho and kacho who will be responsible for implementing the project.

Another characteristic of larger Japanese companies that you should always keep in mind is the problem of direct communication between departments. In some companies there is little or no communication between them—remember the faction mentality. It is almost always advisable, and sometimes critical, for you to develop close working relationships with the managers and assistant managers of several departments and sections to ensure that your project is understood and receives proper treatment by all concerned.

# THE SPIRIT OF
# JAPANESE COMPANIES

EVERY JAPANESE COMPANY of any size has a particular image of itself as well as a company policy that influences its behavior and provides insights into how to approach and deal with it. Familiarity with a company's self-image can therefore be a major asset in approaching it.

There are two key terms used in reference to this company image, which generally includes its character and goals: *shakun* (shah-koon) and *shaze* (shah-zay)—terms that are similar in meaning and more or less interchangeable.

Shaze refers to a company's guidelines for establishing its policies and conducting itself in relation to the community at large as well as the marketplace. The shaze is generally expressed in the form of a motto.

Shakun means something like "company precepts" and refers more specifically to a company's philosophy. It may be written in the form of "commandments" or "house rules."

The shaze/shakun of manufacturers of consumer goods and service companies is particularly important because it is an essential part of their public image, which must be bright, strong, and positive to elicit the right response from the buying public.

A careful study of the shaze/shakun of any company and being able to discuss it in knowledgeable terms can be a big plus for the foreigner from several angles. First, it reveals a great deal about the personality of the company and the role it sees itself playing in the market and world at large. Second, it provides you with useful insights in dealing with the company because it allows you to tailor your approach and relationship to be compatible with, and enhance, the company philosophy and goals.

Showing familiarity with the shakun/shaze of a company at the first meeting can be a very big boost for you in the eyes of your contacts. It demonstrates clearly that you are more than one-dimensional; that you have not just walked in off the street. The Japanese appreciate your having done your homework and are more likely to pay attention to you since you have already, in part at least, qualified yourself as someone who could be a trustworthy contact.

If you do not have a company motto or creed, no matter how small your company might be, you should give some thought to creating one. Actually, the shakun and shaze are as much for the benefit of employees as they are for the public, since they help define company goals, thereby providing employees with guidelines for their own behavior.

By having a company creed you send a strong message to the Japanese that there is an intangible substance to both you and your company, and this helps reduce any stereotyping they may do about you and your firm.

# MAKING THE FIRST CONTACT

It is, of course, important that your first contact with a Japanese company be carefully planned, especially if you initiate the contact. Naturally enough, an ideal scenario is for a Japanese firm to have become aware of and interested in your company from indirect sources, such as a story about your company or project in the news media or one of their own "scouts" or agents picking up on your story and reporting it, resulting in the Japanese side initiating the first approach.

You can make this happen, or at least encourage it, by deliberate action: arranging for news coverage in media most likely to be monitored by the kind of Japanese contact you are looking for, tapping into the information-gathering network of the company you would like to have as a contact and planting the seed that would attract the company to you, exhibiting at trade shows, advertising in the appropriate trade media, and so on.

While there are numerous advantages to having the Japanese side make the first direct move, such as pinpointing the individuals within the company who are involved and shortening the period of time usually consumed by initial steps, it is still essential that you assess any firm that approaches you. Companies attracted by potential new projects may be too small, too big, not well positioned, or in some totally unrelated area, and any prospect should be carefully checked out, including large, well-known companies.

Large companies often look into things in which they have only marginal interest, keep would-be suppliers or partners dangling for months to years, and frequently tie up projects that are not given enough priority to get off the ground floor.

When the first contact is from the Japanese side, the bigger and better known your company, the more likely it is that you will be contacted by at least a bucho (department head). If you are a good-sized company, higher level executives, at least on a director level if your company is really big, are generally brought into the picture when their interest is serious. Depending on the circumstances, the CEO could be brought in, especially in smaller Japanese companies. If they go this far, you can be assured that they have had several meetings about you and have agreed to follow up.

If the company is a major firm and you are introduced to the president or CEO, you should not attempt to make your pitch to them unless you are clearly invited to do so.

When you plan to make the first approach, one tried and proven way is to have a third party, a consultant or agent or other contact (such as a banker), make the initial contact, introduce your company and your project, and get a hearing on whether or not the Japanese side wants to pursue the contact. If they do, obviously they will agree to meet you. This is the category of approach (from the outside) that the Japanese generally prefer because they are far more comfortable in dealing with go-betweens during the early stages of any relationship.

If you prefer for whatever reason to make the first contact on your own, it can be extremely helpful if you do so with an introduction from an individual or company that is well known to your target and in good standing.

It goes without saying that this individual or company should be in a position to give you a shokaijo (introduction) to a specific individual in the right department who has the power to get your proposal an initial hearing.

A letter not addressed to a specific individual or department may find itself in the right hands if the contents are clear, and then again it may not, depending on who gets hold of it first, what they understand of it, and who they think should take care of it. In some cases, their reaction may be based more on internal politics or rivalries than your own best interest.

Larger Japanese companies receive thousands of letters every month, many of them in obscure languages. Most are never answered simply because it would be costly and unproductive to do so.

If you telephone and are unable to specify whom you want to talk to, you will end up having to explain yourself to a receptionist, a clerk, or another low-level member of the General Affairs Department. Depending on their perception of what you want, you can easily be passed around to two, three, or more individuals, in some cases all in the General Affairs Department which screens cold contacts from the outside.

It is common for this department to agree to meet outsiders; listen to their presentations, sometimes spread out over two or three occasions; and then announce that there is no interest in your project or that they will introduce you to the proper department, making it necessary for you to repeat your presentation.

You may not be told directly that there is no interest, since that would be considered impolite. A common reaction is for the Japanese side to say they will consider the idea and then leave you dangling; the assumption being, of course, that your "belly" will tell you what they did not.

Obviously, it is important for you to avoid this kind of situation by determining in advance, or having someone determine for you, whom you should see in a Japanese company.

# GETTING THE STILL
# USEFUL BOW DOWN

**B**OWING is the traditional Japanese form of greeting as well as expressing farewell, appreciation, and sorrow. It is also often the source of awkward and sometimes embarrassing situations between Japanese and foreigners when the foreigners are not familiar with the custom.

Fortunately, the Japanese do not expect foreigners to bow in strictly business situations, and internationalized Japanese, especially those of senior rank, generally no longer bow when they are introduced to foreigners. And in this case, we're talking about fairly deep bows. Nowadays, just a slight head-bow, and maybe a shallow tilt of the upper torso, is appropriate.

There are, however, social and other occasions when the traditional bow is still the order of the day. One thing to keep in mind is that deep bows are reserved for very serious occasions, as when one is apologizing for something, is petitioning for something, or is deeply grateful for something.

For a foreigner to perform a deep bow on other occasions is likely to be taken the wrong way, as it may have comic or idiotic connotations.

116

Most foreigners who have lived in Japan for a number of years absorb the habit of bowing slightly on numerous occasions, generally without thinking about it. If it is natural and not exaggerated, it doesn't hurt, and it might help.

# THE BUSINESS CARD GAME

IN THE traditional Japanese way, bowing and exchanging business cards is done slowly and a bit formally to avoid confusion. Individuals face each other, exchange business cards, glance quickly at the business cards (to see both the name and rank of the other person), and then bow . . . and often shake hands as well.

Foreigners who are not well practiced in Japanese-style greeting formalities often add to the confusion when meeting several people by attempting to bow, shake hands, and pass out business cards at the same time. Again the key is to do it one at a time, slowly, deliberately, with some style.

Business cards are more important in Japan than in most countries because they establish rank as well as identity, and knowledge of rank is vital to the way the Japanese relate to and react to others. But there are some pointers beyond just how to exchange business cards that play a role in overall Japanese business etiquette.

First, it is advisable to have your cards printed in your native language on one side and in phonetic Japanese on the other side. English especially is difficult for Japanese to pronounce because the spelling often doesn't provide enough clues. Having the name of your company, particularly if it is not a well-known name, as well as your title, rendered in Japanese is also important to complete the identification.

Your cards should be well designed and well printed, because this makes a solid, favorable impression. Colored paper stock or other materials are also acceptable and often beneficial—if they are not too far-out. I have been using my photograph on my own cards since the 1950s. It always elicits favorable comments, and beginning in the 1980s a few of the more individualistic Japanese began picking up on the idea. Most Japanese in creative professions have very individualized cards.

It is customary in Japan to use card cases, and this is a practice worth following. Among other things, it keeps your cards from getting dog-eared. A two-compartment case is best—one for yours and one for theirs.

Obviously when you are meeting Japanese, it is both polite and common sense to hand your card to them with the Japanese-language side up and facing them, so they can read it without turning it over or around. Strict etiquette calls for the use of both hands in both giving and receiving cards, at least when you begin the exchange, but it has become common to extend and accept cards with just one hand.

It is not customary for business cards to be put away immediately if you are sitting down or sit down soon after meeting. The practice is to place them on the meeting table in front of you so you can look at the names and titles of the people you've just met to help you remember and use them in your conversation.

Probably the most common breach of business card etiquette committed by foreigners when seated at a meeting table is for them to literally "deal" their cards out as if they were playing poker, tossing or sliding them across tables. Dispensing business cards in this manner may be taken as a demonstration of ignorance of Japanese etiquette or a cavalier attitude toward the Japanese involved ... unless it is done in a very friendly manner, with a smile, and by half-rising out of your chair and bowing a bit at the same time.

If you do not have an opportunity to individually meet your Japanese counterparts before sitting down, you may have to resort to the above ploy.

However, if it is at all practical, the better way is to get up from the table, walk to the other side, and do the exchange directly.

When there are several people in your group, the most efficient way to meet a similar number of Japanese in a conference room is for your group to line up before sitting down, rather than mill around willy nilly and add to the confusion. This uniform, controlled manner of exchanging cards will win you some points.

# GETTING ACQUAINTED

THE DURATION and content of your first meeting will vary depending on who set it up and whether or not the Japanese side already knows something about you and your project. The first few minutes should be kept on a relaxed social level, and then you should express your appreciation for them taking time to see you, say you know how busy they are, and diplomatically ask how much of their time you may have.

If the Japanese side has not been briefed and you are starting from scratch, it is essential that you first identify yourself thoroughly, including a complete explanation of your relationship with the person or people who introduced you to their company, why you have targeted their company in the first place, and lastly the broad outlines of your project or proposition.

If they have already been informed in detail, and particularly if they approached you, you can presume you are talking to the right people and can generally get down to business after a few minutes of pleasantries and getting acquainted.

Presuming that you have your first meeting set up with the right department (in a larger Japanese company), it will generally be with the manager or general manager of the department (these titles are used more or less interchangeably, depending on company policy), with one or more section chiefs, and, depending on the nature of your proposal, people from engineering, marketing and sales, etc.

Once you have described your project in general terms, without asking for or expecting any kind of immediate response from the Japanese side, you should end the first meeting on a light note, commenting that you look forward to meeting with them again after they have had time to consider your proposal—and ask them to set a date for the next meeting.

It is essential that you have your complete proposal in writing, preferably in a bound form with a cover, and leave copies for the Japanese side to study in detail.

There is virtually no chance that the Japanese side will make any kind of decision or commitment on the first hearing of a presentation, other than to look at it carefully and say they will get back to you. With very rare exceptions, such as in entrepreneurial companies still operated by the founder who is a strong one-man manager,

123

individual Japanese, no matter how high their position, do not make decisions on their own. Every subject is discussed at length with all of the managers who would be involved with any aspect of the undertaking, a process that naturally takes time.

The normal routine, when a Japanese company is interested in a project brought in from the outside, is for them to meet several times with the presenters, gradually adding more people to their team or bringing in substitutes until all of their key managers have been involved in the presentation and discussions. This often means that the foreign side must basically make the same presentation several times.

After the Japanese side has heard and/or read all of a proposal, they invariably have questions, sometimes dozens to hundreds of them, depending on the complexity of the project. Different individuals on the Japanese team, who may not attend all of the sessions, often ask the same questions, sometimes phrased a little differently and sometimes not, requiring the foreign side to repeat itself a number of times.

The key to getting through this stage is patience, plus providing the additional information requested as expeditiously as possible and holding as many individual talks as you can with the key section and department chiefs (more about this later). Often, the additional information requested by the Japanese side is something they need for customs, the patent or trademark office, or the ministry concerned with your particular product or service.

This sometimes gets into proprietary areas that are sensitive, and you may want to determine, from outside sources, that the extra information they want is in fact necessary in order for them to abide by government regulations.

# HOW TO RECOGNIZE "NO"

ONE OF the most frustrating experiences the foreigner can have in Japan is to get involved in any kind of presentation or negotiations and not know when he is wasting his time, energy, and money—which happens often.

The genesis of this situation is multifaceted. It begins with the fact that the Japanese usually cannot bring themselves to turn anyone away or turn them down outright with a simple "no, thank you" or "sorry, that's not for us." This situation is then compounded because the unconditioned foreigner does not recognize the subtle verbal and nonverbal clues dropped by the Japanese that mean "No, No, No"—sometimes within minutes of the beginning of a presentation.

Knowing why the Japanese will almost never say "no, thank you" is of no particular help. The key, of course, is picking up on the no-no signals. The most obvious one—and the one that is often the closest to a specific turn-down—is when they say, usually with a strained expression, that something would be *muzukashii* (muu-zuu-kah-she-e), or "difficult." When you hear this, you can bet your last yen that you are not going to get across the moat, much less penetrate the castle.

Sometimes the reaction is expressed nonverbally, in which case you must be a good face-reader and sensitive to voice tones. When traditional Japanese politeness prevents them from going any further than this, they will often end the meeting by saying they will consider your proposition—using the phrase *kangaete okimasu* (kahn-guy-tay oh-kee-mahss), which literally means "I will think about it." It does not mean they will do anything more than just think about it—in other words it is a polite "no."

In the meantime, the Japanese are very much aware that the foreign visitor has not understood their message, because he continues with the pitch, invariably with a degree of enthusiasm and "logical thinking" that repels the Japanese. Thus, the longer the foreigner persists, the stronger the mental block the Japanese build around their fort.

Another sign that a perceptive visitor might pick up on early in the session is that the Japanese side asks no questions and allows him to babble on. When the unperceptive foreigner finally runs down (and some will repeat themselves at the end in a closing pitch), another obvious sign that he has gotten nowhere is when the Japanese do not suggest or readily agree to a follow-up meeting.

Not surprisingly, there are numerous ways of saying "no" with several set phrases: "I'll do my best"; "I'll talk to the senior director about it"; etc. In fact, the word for "no," *iie* (ee-eh), is seldom used in ordinary conversation. In general, the practice is to use the negative form of verbs and other words:

*Ikimasu ka* (E-kee- mahss kah?)—Are you going?
*Ikimasen* (E-kee-mah-sin)—I'm not going.
*Itai desu ka* (Ee-tie dess kah?)—Does it hurt?
*Itaku nai* (Ee-tah-kuu nigh)—It doesn't hurt.

Learning how to "read" meetings with Japanese is not easy, especially when the foreigner is speaking through an interpreter because there is always the additional tendency for the interpreter to soften the impact of any negative comments by the Japanese side. It may be equally difficult when the Japanese side speaks adequate or very good English because they often choose to be even more polite, not using the key words at all and beaming pleasantly throughout the presentation.

It is also very common for foreigners who speak quite good Japanese to become victims of this trap because they are not aware of the specific Japanese psychology and etiquette involved, or because they are unable to escape their own cultural conditioning and accept what they are hearing or seeing. I can personally testify to how easy it is to get emotionally caught up in a project you "know" is right and good and be unable to stop yourself even though you see the red lights and hear the siren.

One of the acceptable ways of finding out if your proposal is alive or dead after about a week to ten days is to call one of the key individuals and ask about it—ask if the interest seems to be serious, if it is moving forward, or if you can provide any additional information to help the process.

Of course, you should make arrangements for this call in advance. Just as your first meeting is ending, you should ask a key member on the Japanese side if it will be alright for you to call or e-mail him a week or so later to find out how it is going.

The follow-up response you get from this contact will almost always tell you how your proposal is faring—if it is actually still on the table and being discussed or if it is dead. A vague, uninformative response almost always means "no."

# THE ROLE OF THE GREETING RITUAL

ONE OF THE MOST important parts of the personal side of business in Japan is the *aisatsu* (aye-sot-sue)—a ritualized greeting that is a significant element in developing and maintaining good relations with clients and business associates.

In its simplest form the aisatsu is just a greeting, the kind in which you would drop by the office of a business associate just to say hello because you happen to be in the neighborhood. The next step up is a visit to offer your congratulations to someone on some auspicious event—a promotion, recovery from an illness, return from an overseas assignment, some laudable business accomplishment, etc., in which case the motive—that of nurturing the relationship in order to obtain or continue some direct benefit—becomes much clearer.

Another important version of aisatsu occurs after outsiders have approached a company on a departmental level and it appears that some kind of a deal is going to be worked out. The Japanese company will generally take the initiative and bring in a director—and in the case of major programs, the president or chairman—for an aisatsu with representatives of the foreign firm.

The most conspicuous and perhaps important use of the aisatsu in keeping business ties tight is at the beginning of each new year when it is a sanctified custom to pay your respects to clients and other valued business contacts, thanking them for their patronage and goodwill the previous year and asking them specifically to continue the relationship during the new year.

This custom is known as *aisatsu mawari* (aye-sot-sue mah-wah-ree), which literally means "greeting go-around." In other words, one goes around from company to company, going through the stylized ritual of bowing to clients and affiliated businessmen, in every case using exactly the same traditional expression: *Saku nen chu ni wa taihen o-sewa ni narimashita. Mata konen mo yoroshiku o-negai itashimasu* (Sah-kuu nane chuu nee wah tie-hane oh-say-wah nee nah-ree-mahssh-tah. Mah-tah kone-nane moe yoe-roe-ssh-kuu oh-nay-gay ee-tah-she-mahss). This translates loosely as, "We are deeply obligated to you for your patronage or support/help last year. We humbly ask that you favor us again this year."

This is a custom which foreigners can quickly adopt in their relations with the Japanese. It requires no special expertise (the greeting can be in English for that matter), and it is very mean- ingful to the Japanese because it demonstrates to them your sincerity and reassures them that you are a person who can be trusted to do what is right at the right time. Of course, it is even more impressive if you learn the above set phrase in Japanese and use it at the appropriate time.

# SEEING BEHIND THE FACADE

IN Japanese culture the practice of "putting on a face" for the public, of concealing your real thoughts behind a carefully constructed facade of dress and protocol, has been one of the key facets of life. The foundation for this type of behavior was laid during the long feudal period when interpersonal relations were strictly governed by meticulously graded class and rank and an even more meticulously detailed etiquette that applied to virtually every act of life.

Presenting the right kind of "face" at the right time was vital to survival in a very literal sense, so people became masters at masking their feelings and their true desires behind a public facade or the already-mentioned tatemae, which originally meant the ceremonial erection of the framework of a house.

In a business sense, tatemae refers to the public image that one presents to outsiders, whether in a negotiating session or just in general. One of the keys to succeeding in business in Japan is to develop considerable skill in seeing behind the tatemae to determine the real situation—what the individual concerned really wants.

A tatemae front is used by the Japanese to conceal negative factors or to cover up actions or events they do not want to reveal or do openly. Recognizing and understanding this ploy requires even more experience and cultural sensitivity.

Of course, just about everybody postures and puts on an act that is tatemae, but generally far less so than the Japanese. The typical Western businessman, for example, is generally motivated by a high sense of fairness and prides himself on being candid—putting all of his cards on the table, as the saying goes.

Not so the Japanese. They are conditioned to reveal as little as they can about their intentions, often concealed behind a sophisticated facade, until they find out as much as possible about what the other side wants and also until they determine where the consensus lies within their own group, since they do not want to be seen as being out of step.

Tatemae could also be described as the world presented through rose-colored glasses, carefully crafted for the outsider's benefit. Extrapolating a little further, the Japan that most foreigners see is a masterpiece of tatemae that hides a very different reality.

There is generally no fast, direct way one can get behind a tatemae and discern the true feelings or intentions of a Japanese negotiating team or individual Japanese during the first and early stages of an encounter. But the facade is not necessarily meant to deceive. It is also used simply to "cover" things until "reality" emerges from the consensus process.

Once you do get past tatemae, or your Japanese contacts reach the stage where they themselves discard the facade and reveal the true situation to you, you have reached honne, or the "honest voice." Achieving honne in your relations with Japanese businesses is very much like pursuing enlightenment. It is often not so much a verbal process as an intuitive or visceral process which just grows on you.

It often happens that virtually all you see and hear in your daytime dealings with Japanese is tatemae. Honne often comes into play outside of office hours and often at night when you are out on the town.

# THE ALL-IMPORTANT
# PRE-AGREEMENT MEETINGS

**J**APANESE CONCERN with interpersonal harmony, and especially avoiding public displays of disagreement, led to the development of what is known as *uchiawase* (uu-chee-ah-wah-say), figuratively "coming to agreement in advance," as a vital part of all social and work activity.

In the social sense, this is nothing more than advance planning, which everyone does, but when applied to business, particularly to business with foreign companies, it becomes part of the negotiating process that foreigners need to know about.

All business projects in Japan, of whatever nature, are preceded by one or more (and usually it is more) uchiawase, which is the key reason why it is so important to provide a Japanese company with all the pertinent information possible prior to meeting them to negotiate any kind of arrangement. The more information they have been given and the stronger it presents your project, the more likely you are to achieve your goals.

The Japanese way is to settle all of the issues of any project during the uchiawase stage—which, again, is why they ask for so much information in advance—and then come together officially for formal recognition of the agreement. Foreigners who are aware of what is going on in the background can help their own case by making themselves available for—and requesting—unofficial meetings, including evenings out in the mizu shobai during this period.

After an agreement is reached, Japanese businessmen traditionally celebrate with an *uchiage* (uu-chee-ah-gay), which literally means "shoot off," as in fireworks, but in this case means more like "send off," in terms of the project to be launched. In the old days this ceremony always included the ritual clapping of hands in a rhythmic cadence, along with a lot of drinking. Now the hand-clapping may be skipped, but not the drinking.

# REVOLVING THE ROOTS

THE UCHIAWASE PROCESS is part of Japan's group- or team-oriented approach to decision-making by consensus that is known in its entirety as *nemawashi* (nay-mah-wah-she), which literally means "root revolving," or the spinning or turning of a root to make sure that it will spread out, "take root," and grow.

The inference in this term is that the proposed project or subject of discussion (the root) is "revolved" (or spun or turned) around and around by all of the people concerned until they have become thoroughly familiar with it, have asked all the questions they might have, and made all of the suggestions they might want to make—or come out against the project.

This is the aspect of decision-making in Japan that often confuses and frustrates foreigners, because it takes so long and because it is often impossible for anyone to say how the project is faring at any one time or stage because there are so many people involved in the "spinning" process that no individual knows exactly where it stands.

Generally, the most important people in the early stages of the nemawashi process are the kacho (section chiefs), who are the ones usually responsible for doing all of the staff work, the research, and the recommendations to higher level management. Sometimes, particularly in the case of a major project in which the involvement of the company would be on a large scale, the man in charge of the project may be a deputy department chief or department head (the equivalent of a vice president in Western terms).

Often it is only during the uchiawase/nemawashi process that the outsider can bring influence to bear on the decision-making process. That is the reason why it is vital that the Japanese side have all the pertinent information about a project, and that they understand it completely—and why it is important to stay in close—usually unofficial—contact with key individuals during this process, meetings over lunch, dinner or drinks, etc., to add more insights, more ammunition, without being pushy. If you come on too strong, you can do more damage than good.

During the uchiawase/nemawashi process the foreigner may be faced with statements from the Japanese side while trying to find out the status of a project that are unintentionally misleading. Two main pitfalls are "I will do my best" and "I understand" which we will explore next.

# I WILL DO MY BEST

A CULTURAL TRAP that many foreign politicians, diplomats, and businessmen have stepped into in their dealings with Japan is bound up in the common expression *zensho shimasu* (zen-show she-mahss), which is sometimes translated as "I will do my best" and other times as "I will take care of it."

The meaning intended when this phrase is used is not always clear from the context of the conversation, and therein lies the rub. A person who is asked to do something may respond enthusiastically with zensho shimasu. If the hearer accepts this as meaning "I will take care of it," while the speaker means "I will do my best," both parties may be confused as well as put out by the mutual misunderstandings that can occur.

A Japanese speaker will use the "I will do my best" version of zensho shimasu when he knows full well that he cannot or does not plan to do anything, without intending to deceive the other party. What he does do is leave it up to the other party to divine the real meaning and the reasons why he responded with this ambiguous term and to accept them without getting mad.

This is another situation where the foreigner who is not truly plugged into the Japanese wavelength must resort to getting help from someone else who can decode the message for him.

There are, in fact, other forms of Japanese communication that are quite different from the Western way. It is a regular custom for Japanese to just begin a sentence and leave two-thirds or more of it unsaid for the listener to fill in.

This is one of the reasons why linguistic experts in Japan say that the Japanese typically understand only about 80 percent of what they hear the first time around.

Given this added aspect of communicating in Japan, you must at all times go the extra mile in making sure that you are understanding and being understood by your Japanese contacts and associates.

# I UNDERSTAND YOU

As USED in Japan, "I understand you" is another of those cultural abysses into which one can fall, suffering slide burns on the way down and a mighty jolt when you hit bottom. It is so basic and so important that it should always be uppermost in your mind.

It is a cultural habit of the Japanese to say, *Hai, wakarimasu* (Hie, wah-kah-ree-mahss), "Yes, I understand," or the past tense, *Hai, wakarimashita* (Hie, wah-kah-ree-mahssh-tah), "I understood (what you said)," in situations where the foreigner habitually takes it as an affirmative response and has the impression that some action is going to be initiated.

There are occasions when this phrase means the same in English as it does in Japanese. There are occasions when it does mean that the individual responding is going to do what he was told to do or what he was asked to consider (and do)—as in a project presentation.

Often, however, when foreigners make presentations or request things, Japanese will respond with this phrase when it just means that they heard and understood—not that they are going to do anything. On these occasions, using the term is another way of delaying things or brushing them aside altogether.

The challenge, of course, is to interpret the response correctly. If it is, in fact, an affirmative reply and action is going to be taken, you can usually determine this by an additional question or two regarding time or scheduling.

At this point, if the response is unclear or noncommittal, you have your answer.

# THE WRITTEN
# DOCUMENT SYSTEM

Once the section chiefs
and department managers have done their
thing, their proposals or recommendations are
put into written form and passed on to their
counterparts in other sections or departments
who in turn add their comments if any and pass
them on.

Generally, all of the section chiefs, all of the
deputy department chiefs, and all of the department chiefs who would be involved in implementing any aspect of the proposal get their turn
at the document.

In earlier years, the written form of a proposal
was generally referred to as a *ringi sho* (reen-ghee
show), or "written document," and the process was
known as the *ringi seido* (reen-ghee say-e-doe), or
"written document system" or "request for decision
system."

It was a very formal affair in which each par-
ticipant had to sign off on each document with
his official name stamp or *hanko* (hahn-koe).
Those who disapproved of the proposal would
refuse to stamp it; if they were not totally

opposed but had strong reservations, they would put their stamp on upside down.

Over the years this process has become less bureaucratic in most companies, some no longer refer to the process they use as the ringi system, and some hold meetings instead of circulating documents. But the process of approval or disapproval of a proposal remains essentially the same- it must be presented to all concerned, in all of its ramifications, and virtually unanimous agreement must be achieved before it is accepted.

Once again the most critical period of any project being considered by a Japanese company—no matter where it comes from—is when the kacho (who may include engineers, etc.) are doing their research, planning, and drafting of whatever proposal they are going to make. If the proposal has come from the outside, this is the point at which it is vital to make sure that the person in charge has every possible detail and insight that you can provide.

It is therefore extremely important to find out, in advance, from the initiating section chief or deputy department chief who the other key people are in the process—whom he will be circulating the proposal to or holding meetings with on his level—so that you can also meet them and—without being too forward—do your best to make sure they also have all of the pertinent facts as you see them before they reach the final stage of decision-making.

If your relationship with the key "window man" is good (if he obviously appreciates the potential of the project and is pursuing it diligently), he will be very cooperative as far as getting input from you is concerned and will generally cooperate in introducing you to the other players, since having committed himself to some degree, he will also have a vested interest in getting the approval of his colleagues.

In going beyond the "window man," however, you must exercise extreme caution not to undercut him or in any way give the impression that you are going around or over him. Any such action or impression will invariably result in his losing face and will sour your relationship with him.

While on the subject of written proposals, it should be noted that Japanese businessmen write very few memos or letters—because of the complexity of the Japanese language and the difficulty of writing it, most companies do not employ secretaries in the Western sense and most Japanese executives prefer to manage with the spoken word and direct face-to-face contact instead of cold type.

All this combined is, of course, why the Japanese have so many meetings in the course of a business day and also part of the reason why they prefer large "open" offices, without separate compartments or dividers, in which everybody in the place can be seen and where communication can circulate freely throughout the room more or less at the same time, with everyone knowing what the others are doing, how they are behaving, and whom they are meeting.

# THE IMPORTANCE OF
# FOLLOWING UP

ONCE you have made an approach to a Japanese company, it is essential that you follow up in a systematic and deliberate way. This, of course, demonstrates the level of your interest, but more importantly it is usually necessary for you to continue providing positive input.

As mentioned earlier, going through your main contact man to his counterparts in other sections and departments is often the key to getting the consensus you want.

Many foreigners who go to Japan to make presentations fail to do sufficient follow-up after their return home either because they think there is nothing more for them to say or because they believe the next step is up to the Japanese side. The point is that failure to keep regular contact with a potential Japanese customer or partner results in a kind of vacuum in which you may be forgotten and action may wind down and possibly stop altogether. At the very least, it is likely to take on a color that is more to the liking of the Japanese.

The Japanese do not feel comfortable or confident in a relationship unless there is frequent, personal contact, especially in the first stages of a budding new relationship. To prevent the creation of a gap, it is important that you have some kind of contact at least every week until the bonds are well cemented. This contact can be a phone call, an e-mail, a fax, in person, or a combination.

Nowadays, a fax or e-mail is generally preferable to a phone call because you can say exactly what you want and there is a record of your comments. These follow-ups can include such things as additional information that relates to your joint interests or expressions of your readiness to provide such information should they need or want it.

In dealing with the Japanese it is important to keep in mind that business there is done on a very personal level and that the Japanese are a very emotional and sensitive people who need to be stroked regularly. There are a number of institutionalized customs designed specifically to meet these emotional needs, which will be discussed later.

# HOW TO USE INTERPRETERS

USING *tsuyaku* (t'sue-yah-kuu), or interpreters, effectively requires a considerable amount of skill that usually comes only with experience. But being forewarned will significantly shorten this learning curve.

First, it is important that the foreigner understand and accept the fact that good interpreting on such important issues as business and politics is very difficult and demanding, and that really first-rate interpreters are exceedingly rare.

A second important point to keep in mind is that as long as it is the Japanese side that provides the interpreter, you are at a disadvantage that ranges from moderate to very serious.

When the interpreter belongs to the other side, over and above the fact that he or she may not really be good at it and may fail to fully transmits what each side says, you must keep in mind that the nonprofessionally trained interpreter will to varying degrees "reinterpret" what both sides say, especially what the foreign side says, to suit his or her own position, habits, beliefs, aims, and often social rank in relation to the Japanese side.

A Japanese interpreter provided by the Japanese side will also be under significant etiquette constraints to "sanitize" the conversation to avoid upsetting anyone, often thereby failing to translate both meanings and feelings—leaving both sides dissatisfied since they readily recognize from the tone of voice and by face-reading that there is some passion involved.

The first rule in using interpreters is therefore to provide your own whenever humanly possible. The second rule is that regardless of whose interpreter you are using, it is very important that you talk with them at length before the beginning of any meeting, not only to judge the level of their ability, but especially to brief them in as much detail as possible about the subject matter you are going to cover.

Just lecturing them and having them nod and say yes is usually not enough. You should ask them to at least verbally summarize the main points to make sure they do in fact understand what you are talking about.

Ideally, you would be able to provide interpreters with a written version of your presentations in advance. You should then question them closely to make sure they understand it in your language. If you must, in fact, depend upon interpreters provided by the Japanese side, you should not hesitate to request that you be permitted to meet them before the beginning of any meeting to discuss your material.

If an individual assigned by a Japanese company to act as interpreter does not want to meet you, is reluctant to do so, or is prevented from doing so, you are already in trouble.

There is a tendency for people to overuse interpreters and tire them out, no doubt presuming that it is easy work—just talking. But doing a thoroughly professional job of interpreting is one of the most demanding intellectual and emotional exercises one can engage in. Sessions should not go beyond two hours without breaks. For daylong programs you should have a minimum of two interpreters so they can spell each other.

Another thing to avoid is attempts at canned humor, especially ethnic jokes which often do not translate well even when the interpreter is a master. Spontaneous humor, on the other hand, especially the self-deprecating kind, is just as much appreciated in Japan as anywhere else, and an appropriate remark that fits the occasion can get you just as much mileage.

154

# MORE ON FAILING
# TO FOLLOW THROUGH

ONE OF THE biggest weaknesses of foreigners attempting to initiate a relationship with Japanese companies is failure to follow through after the first meetings. This lapse derives from a combination of factors that, of course, come under the general heading of lack of knowledge about the way the Japanese do business.

This lack particularly applies to those who assume that all they have to do is inform the Japanese side of a good business deal or area of potential and then sit back and wait for the Japanese to pick up the ball and run with it. That can happen, but generally it does not. Not having an established business relationship with the foreign company to begin with can be enough by itself to stop the Japanese side from taking any action, even when they find the proposition interesting.

The Japanese side expects the foreign company to follow-up on a regular, consistent, comprehensive basis and to take all the steps they believe are necessary to establish an acceptable relationship, providing them with all of the assurances and evidence they need to accept the foreign firm as a stable, trustworthy company they can deal with in confidence.

Another aspect of the problem is that foreigners inexperienced in Japan are not aware of the personal factor in Japanese business relations: of how much personal time must be invested in establishing a business relationship. It does not begin and end with a good product and good price. These come after the personal ties are formed.

It is vital for the foreign side to keep in mind that initiating and nurturing a successful new business relationship with a Japanese company is something like planting and growing some kind of fragile flower that requires regular, and sometimes daily, care.

It is also like a marriage that breaks down quickly if the couple does not communicate and stroke each other regularly.

Another problem that often accompanies the failure to follow through syndrome is lack of sufficient research and preparation prior to the first contact. The Japanese will research a project for six months or more before making the decision to do it, but once the decision is made, they are prepared to implement it immediately.

In contrast to this, foreigners, and especially Americans it seems, will announce new projects and then spend six months or more researching and preparing before they are ready to start them.

When foreign companies hooked on this method approach a Japanese firm, which turns out to be interested, they often find themselves needing six months or more study and preparation before they can meet the expectations of the Japanese. This naturally suggests to the Japanese side that the foreign company is short-sighted, if not incompetent, and could well put a damper on their interest.

The message is: do your homework; make the contact; follow up as diligently and as frequently as you would in courting a very desirable mate.

# DEALING AT THE NEGOTIATING TABLE

AFTER an agreement is reached and a foreign company begins to do business with a Japanese company, situations requiring additional negotiation invariably arise—either from the foreign side or the Japanese side, or both. When the foreign side raises questions, it is naturally their responsibility to state their case. When both sides mutually agree more or less simultaneously that another negotiation session is needed, the Japanese side will generally invite—or insist—that the foreign side present their case first.

On the surface this may be offered as a gesture of courtesy—giving the other side the first shot. But in reality it is a well-practiced ploy to achieve an advantage, since it allows the Japanese side to adjust their responses in their favor.

When you are the initiator, the best negotiating approach is to first cover the points in general, broad terms, letting the framework of what you propose sink in. Once this is done, you may or may not get any feedback from the Japanese side.

They may say they cannot comment until they get more details.

On your second run-through, when you do go into more specifics, you should open each main point up for discussion, pulling the Japanese side in and questioning them to draw out their thinking on each item.

It is important that you make any presentation slowly and clearly, using graphics and other supporting materials as much as possible, and that someone in your group keeps track of all the questions the Japanese side asks, as well as your answers. Invariably on the Japanese side there will be one or more people who do not participate in the dialogue and do nothing but scribble notes, making it possible for them to thoroughly review the proceedings afterward.

Surprisingly, many foreigners negotiating in Japan ask few if any questions of their Japanese opposites—sometimes, it seems, out of a misplaced sense of politeness. You should go into every session with a written list of questions to ask and add to the list as the negotiations proceed.

In fact, one of the reasons why so many foreign companies have problems with their

Japanese partners after they go into business together is that the foreign side did not ask enough questions during the courting stage. This is often serious and can be fatal.

# KILLING WITH SILENCE

IN JAPANESE negotiating protocol, long periods of silence are a part of the process. They are both a brief, unannounced, unofficial rest period as well as a strategic ploy during which both sides continue to feel each other out nonverbally. Members of the Japanese team will simply stop talking. Some will lean back and close their eyes, as if sleeping.

Members of the group will often get up and leave the table, returning to their desks or going to the toilet or whatever, without any sign. They will also hold whispered or low-voiced consultations in Japanese with other members of the team—especially when there is no one on the foreign side that understands Japanese.

The tactical aspect of this practice is known as *maku satsu* (mah-kuu sot-sue), which is usually translated as "killing with silence." The Japanese negotiators will go silent as a technique for drawing the other side out, to get them to give in to a point or make other concessions.

Americans in particular seem to be especially susceptible to this tactic. Being aggressive and conditioned to expect things to move forward rapidly in clockwork fashion, they become increasingly uncomfortable even with a silence of only a few seconds and begin talking, usually repeating themselves and often making concessions outright or hinting that their position is not cut in stone. A silence of thirty seconds or so is enough to make many American negotiators panic.

The proper response to the maku satsu ploy is to review your notes, refresh yourself if you need to, chat privately with a member of your own team, and let the scenario develop for four or five minutes. When the Japanese see that you are familiar with the strategy and are not going to give the store away, they will usually resume the discussions. Or, after sufficient time has elapsed for you to make your point (that you also know the art of maku satsu), you can take the initiative and resume the meeting without losing any ground.

Another aspect of the use of time: foreign negotiators should not announce that they have a deadline and will be leaving on such-and-such a date. This gives the Japanese side the opportunity to bring increasing pressure on the foreign side simply by delaying things. The closer the deadline comes, the more apt the foreign side is to give in and accept the Japanese position. I have been involved in situations (not from the beginning!) in which the last points were agreed upon in a car on the way to the airport.

You can certainly let the Japanese know that time is important and that, if you cannot work out an acceptable relationship with them, you will go on to other prospects. But don't lock yourself in to where you have to accept what is offered because you have planned to stay in Japan for only four or five days.

# BEWARE OF USING LOGIC

IN SOME FIFTY YEARS of living and working with Japanese, I have been faulted hundreds of times for trying to conduct myself in a logical manner—for almost always assuming that any successful business is based on the principle that fact follows fact; that two plus two always equals four. In Japan that is often not so.

In fact, the Japanese are often made very uncomfortable by naked logical thinking. In the Japanese context, feeling is often more important than logical reasoning. They believe that an enterprise based only on logical thinking cannot give proper due to the human element—recognizing, it seems, that human beings are generally illogical creatures.

To the Japanese, when people have their "logic cap" on, they are incapable of "heart-to-heart" communication and cannot use the "art of the belly." The Japanese equate logical thinking with independent thinking and independent thinking with an inability to cooperate with others in a Japanese-style team effort.

The foreigner who stands up and uses good, solid logic to preach a sermon about the merits of his product or project is on safe enough ground. But he is soon in quicksand if he uses the same approach in proposing how the enterprise should be launched and managed. About the only effective solution is to downplay "cold, hard reasoning" in all discussions, but quietly mix as much logic as possible in with the Japanese approach when implementing a project.

Arguing a business point with the Japanese on the basis of pure reasoning—something Americans are particularly prone to do—is sometimes enough to make some of them go silent (blow a fuse) if you push it too strongly. A gambit that often proves effective is to cloak your logical argument in very human, personal terms, approaching it from the side or the back instead of straight on.

# MASTERING THE ART OF DOING BUSINESS AT NIGHT

ONE OF THE MOST interesting aspects of business in Japan—and another key to doing it successfully that I have already mentioned several times—is what has traditionally been known as the mizu shobai, or "water business," which refers primarily to the nighttime entertainment trades—hostess bars, night clubs, geisha inns, and hot bath massage parlors, etc.

Both business and politics in Japan have long been associated with the mizu shobai, with deals planned and consummated in a mizu shobai setting instead of in an office or boardroom. One reason for this is that in the old days, private offices were virtually nonexistent, and if one wanted to talk privately, it was often better that it be done in a public place. Another reason is that the drinking of sake, the traditional Japanese alcoholic beverage, has also long been directly associated with formal events and ceremonies (just as alcoholic drinks have in Western societies) as a semi-sacred ritual that formalized decisions or actions.

A third factor is that the traditionally strict etiquette that prevailed in Japan made it either difficult or impossible for the Japanese to talk freely and frankly except when they were in recognized, sanctioned drinking places, could forget about tatemae and really let their hair down. Japanese history is filled with anecdotes about famed political and business leaders meeting in red-light districts and geisha inns to carry on their business.

Those purveyors of sensual pleasure apparently symbolized the intimate nature of the relationship they desired.

The role of the mizu shobai in politics and business in present-day Japan has diminished somewhat, but the venue for businessmen is usually an exclusive bar, a private club, or hostess bar.

The change that overcomes the typical Japanese businessman in a hostess bar, with its cadre of attractive hostesses and intimate ambiance, is startling to see. From the formal, protocol-conscious organization man who behaves in a meticulously prescribed manner, the businessman becomes a lighthearted playboy. He drinks, laughs, sings, dances, and often behaves in a licentious manner toward the hostess bar girls.

It is in the mizu shobai that Japanese cement and maintain the personal ties and emotional bonds that are so important to their business relationships. They do not—virtually cannot—feel at ease with another person or feel that they know them and can trust them until they have shared a number of hostess bar, bathhouse, or geisha house experiences because it is only on these occasions that they allow their own personal feelings and character to come out, and they presume it is the same with non-Japanese as well.

The ritual of drinking and letting go in the "water trade" is so important to the Japanese that even those who are not heavy drinkers and dedicated carousers will simulate the behavior in order to fit in, be accepted, and play the necessary game.

Foreigners who become involved with the Japanese are invariably invited to a hostess bar or inn that calls in geisha. Where visitors from abroad are concerned, the first invitation is usually on the second or third day, after the visitors have had a good night's sleep and a day or so of meetings—during which decisions and/or judgments are only rarely made.

168

What often happens is that about two or three hours into the evening at a hostess bar, or other night spot—and sometimes just as the party is near the end—one of the Japanese will suddenly sober up and very directly and pointedly comment on the negotiations, either that they are going well or that there is a problem or obstacle that has to be overcome.

The Japanese side does not expect the foreign side to immediately launch into an impromptu meeting and start discussions. They are letting the foreign side know what is going on so the foreigner can think about it overnight and react to it the following day.

As soon as these brief comments are made—usually in a minute or so—the Japanese will instantly revert to the role of playboy on the town, without missing a beat.

# THE IMPORTANCE OF A HIDDEN ART

THERE IS ONE key to doing business in Japan that can be a lot of fun if the foreigner will just put his or her heart (and a few other things) into it. This facet of the Japanese business world is known as *kakushi gei* (kah-kuu-she gay-e), or "hidden art," and refers to some personal skill—usually singing—which the individual businessperson can demonstrate in public.

As already mentioned in the section on the mizu shobai, Japanese businesspeople spend a lot of time in bars and pubs. One of the most popular category of nightspots are the karaoke bars or lounges, where patrons are encouraged to take center stage and sing into a microphone in sync with piped in orchestra music.

In earlier times, learning how to sing was a part of the growing up and educational process in Japan. Mothers taught children how to sing, and singing was practiced in school. People sang at parties, at festivals, and at special ceremonies, in groups and individually. Most Japanese still do a lot of singing during their formative years, and almost any businessman has at least the courage if not the skill to stand up and sing a solo when the occasion arises.

But not content with just being a so-so singer, many Japanese practice discreetly, developing their kakushi gei so that when they are called on to sing or when they volunteer to sing they will not be embarrassed and their friends and coworkers will be pleasantly impressed.

There is probably not one lower- or middle-ranking manager in Japan who has not patronized a karaoke bar and taken his turn on the floor, crooning his most practiced tune. And visiting foreigners are expected to take their turns as well! In fact, "forced to take their turns" may be a more accurate term, since Japanese hosts can be extraordinarily aggressive when living it up in singing bars.

Of course, the Japanese assume that all foreigners can sing at least as well as they can and have no special fears about getting up and performing in public. So saying no to an insistent host (whom you want to do business with) is very difficult.

To the Japanese businessman, carrying on and singing in a karaoke bar is therapy—therapy that he sorely needs to mitigate the strict behavior required of him during the day and the massive pressure he must face inside the Japanese system. It is, in fact, a marvelous way to eliminate stress.

I remember my own first experience in a singing bar. I resisted heroically because I cannot carry a tune, didn't know the words to any song, and was shy about making an utter fool of myself.

My Japanese hosts simply would not let me off the hook, however, and finally one of them agreed to join me in a duo. We were given a songbook so I was able to read the words and struggle through. Despite the embarrassment, it was a very satisfying experience, and I was immensely pleased with myself (the drunken audience applauded loudly).

You can avoid a great deal of the embarrassment I went through, have much more fun, and impress your Japanese contacts favorably by learning a couple of popular ballads and willingly belting them out with gusto at the first invitation.

# "NOMI-NICATION": GATHERING WISDOM IN BARS

ANOTHER facet of the Japanese custom of using hostess bars and other mizu shobai facilities in conducting business is one that is described by the word "nomi-nication"— a term coined in the 1970s. Nomi (no-me) means "drink" in Japanese. When combined with the latter half of "communication," you have a form of communicating through drinking.

As we have already learned, it is conventional wisdom in Japan that a person reveals his or her true self only when drunk and that you can get to really know a person only when they are in a state of inebriation. Given this situation— generally true in Japan because sober-time etiquette precludes "honest" behavior on other occasions it is simply mandatory that the Japanese get together and drink in order to really get acquainted and find out what they actually think about things, business matters included.

In other words, if this situation is accepted as basically fact, the Japanese would not be able to succeed in business without regularly hitting the bottle with their coworkers. Experience has proven that it is true to some extent.

Many Japanese businessmen have told me directly that their whole approach to maintaining effective employee relations, developing and using business contacts, and "gathering wisdom" was done through or while drinking.

Certainly not all Japanese businessmen go quite that far, but there is no doubt that "nomination" is a vital part of the business process in Japan and is therefore an important skill foreign businesspersons should learn.

Virtually all Japanese businessmen and women have two or three *yukitsuke no ba* (yuu-kee-skay no bah), or "favorite bars," where they regularly take associates and guests for business conversations. It is recommended that foreign business-people have their own yukitsuke no ba or clubs for the same purpose.

# LET'S HAVE A DRINK

IF YOU WANT to get acquainted with a Japanese businessman for whatever purpose, or have a "heart-to-heart" talk with a businessman you already know, neither your office nor his office is the place to do it. There are a number of reasons for this—one being that few Japanese businessmen have private offices and holding such meetings in conference rooms is not appropriate. The most important reason, however, is that the "personal side" of business has traditionally been pursued outside the office—at coffee shops, restaurants, or bar-lounges (as opposed to hostess bars).

A signal that someone wants to get to know you or talk to you seriously about anything, including business, is an invitation to meet outside the office. This invitation is often made in the form of the stock phrase *Ippai yarimasho!* (Eep-pie yah-ree-mah-show!).

This literally means "Let's do a full one (cup or glass)." In other words, "Let's have a drink." When addressing a foreigner, however, the invitation may be couched in more elegant terms.

This is an institutionalized facet of the business process in Japan, and one that you can also use. It is best done in the evening and may include drinks and dinner or just drinks if it ends by around seven o'clock. The best places for such meetings are the lounges of hotels, conveniently located for public transportation, or private clubs.

Generally speaking, it is the lower- and middle-ranked managers who will most readily respond to such invitations (if they decline twice in a row, you can assume you are not on their approved list), often depending on your age and your rank/position in relation to theirs. The closer you are to their age and rank, or if you are higher and there are no other negatives, the more likely they will accept such an invitation.

In the case of upper-level and top management, it would not be considered appropriate for you to invite them out unless you are approximately the same age and rank. The higher the rank of the individual you invite out, the more prestigious the meeting place should be. Those in the upper stratosphere normally go only to private clubs or exclusive restaurants with private rooms for such meetings—not hotels, hostess bars, etc.

If you have no choice but to use a hotel and your guest is to be someone of high rank in a

major company or ministry, it would be appropriate to engage a private suite. (Some hotels in
Japan have such suites for that specific purpose,
usually as part of their business centers.)

Many foreign businesspeople stationed in Tokyo
have found such after-hours meetings the ideal
way to communicate on a very personal level with
their Japanese counterparts. Not only does it allow
them to have a much more congenial relationship
with their Japanese colleagues, it also relieves
much of the cultural stress one is subjected to in
doing business in Japan.

# BUSINESS ON THE GREENS

THERE IS another facet of doing business in Japan that is more familiar to Westerners and generally more acceptable to them than the age-old mizu shobai approach—namely, cementing personal relations and doing business on the golf course. As soon as the Japanese became aware of the role of golf in business in the U.S. in the late 1950s and 1960s, they took to it with the same obsessive dedication they exhibit toward any serious enterprise.

Membership in a golf course became an important business asset and a symbol of internationalism. Net-enclosed practice ranges sprang up on tiny vacant lots, on the tops of buildings, and in other unlikely places. Hundreds of thousands of Japanese men of all ages began spending part of their Sundays learning how to swing a golf club as part of their business skills.

For most present-day Japanese businessmen, to admit that they do not belong to a golf club or do not play golf is like confessing to a serious failing in their professional training.

Although differing radically from the mizu shobai, particularly in that it is a Western practice

178

and is far removed from traditional Japanese behavior, the golf course has nevertheless been integrated into the Japanese business system on a par with hostess bars and geisha inns—providing Western businessmen with an opportunity to do business with the Japanese on equal if not advantageous terms.

A golf course is a golf course whether it is in Japan or not. Being a Western game with its own rules of conduct based on individual action and behavior, golf (unlike baseball) cannot be Japanized. The foreigner does not have to know Japanese protocol to play golf with Japanese businessmen. On the contrary, it is the Japanese who must change their traditional behavior to conform to "golf etiquette."

Of course, one doesn't talk about business while actually playing golf. When and if done directly, such discussions take place in the clubhouse after the game is over. The primary role of the golf course is to provide an opportunity for the two sides to participate in a joint activity that helps them get to know one another and form personal ties that lead to agreements outside of the strict protocol of formal office and conference room meetings.

179

Japanese businessmen who do business with foreigners generally have two "modes" of operation—a Japanese mode and a foreign mode. When they are dealing with foreigners, their attitudes and behavior undergo changes that range from subtle to drastic. When they are in their own offices in Japan, surrounded by their coworkers, these changes are very subtle and often do not appreciably change the end result of their dealings with foreigners. The further they get away from their own office environment, however, the more significant the change.

To the Japanese, cultural behavior is intimately related to their physical surroundings. In a Japanese setting they will behave in a traditional Japanese way. In foreign settings, they tend to behave in the manner which they think is appropriate for that particular setting. Their behavior on a golf course in Japan—a Western setting—differs from their office behavior. Their behavior on a golf course outside of Japan differs even more, because the setting is less Japanese.

Foreigners can take significant advantage of this chameleon factor in the Japanese character to help level the playing field when they engage in business with the Japanese. In other words, the more business talks and negotiations you can have outside the home office of the Japanese, the better, and the more often these outside locations can be in Western settings, the more advantage you will have.

Of course, I am not suggesting that you set up tables and chairs on a golf course and engage in full fledged negotiations on the greens. But golf courses, as well as other strictly Western scenarios, are the foreign equivalent of the hostess bar, when the Japanese way is to stop singing or carousing for just seconds or minutes to make their business position and/or requirements clear. These little business interludes should be well planned and deliberately but deftly executed.

The idea is to shift your manner and behavior entirely for just the brief period that you are in a business mode, going from very casual to very serious. This sudden shift will alert the Japanese antenna that an important message is coming in, and since this is the way they operate, it should be loud and clear.

# A DASH OF CULTURE

IT HAS BEEN SAID that the religion of present-day Japan is business, which is pursued with an evangelism that verges on the demonic. But because of Japan's long history steeped in Confucianism, Daoism, and Buddhism, there is a philosophical streak in most Japanese that begins to emerge and flower as they grow older, particularly in men and especially so the more successful they are.

The businessman-philosopher is certainly not unknown in the West, but he is the exception rather than the rule. In Japan, on the other hand, the final stage for virtually every successful businessman is that of the philosopher—as if the transformation was preordained. The nature of business management in Japan is a reflection of this phenomenon.

The higher-level executive is expected to withdraw more and more from daily company activities as he moves up the managerial ladder and to become a sage—the company's philosophical and spiritual guide.

The historical traditions of the West, as well as contemporary management practices, in particular the musical chairs movement of executives among companies, generally preclude the development of the type of loyalty and security that is necessary to inspire and sustain a philosophical concern for either company or country. Western businesspeople are therefore apt to be handicapped on this aspect in their dealings with the Japanese.

One of the ways to mitigate this weakness is to inject a conspicuously cultural element into your business relationships with the Japanese. This element may involve art, handicrafts, music, literature, or other cultural expressions or combinations of them. Such concern and involvement lowers the obsession with material things and puts the practice of business on a more personal level—something that the Japanese appreciate and believe to be morally right.

One American businessman stationed in Japan for many years gained a lot of mileage with his counterparts as the result of becoming a collector of pottery and something of an authority on its history in Japan. This alone took him out of the admittedly stereotyped image of the foreigner in Japan and gave him a cultural tie with the Japanese that helped him transcend the differences that separated them.

Another foreigner of my acquaintance achieved the same results from his interest and involvement in woodblock prints. Still another turned a strong interest in the writings of contemporary Japanese businessmen into a valuable asset in his relationships in Japan (reaching the point where he was invited to lecture on the differences between Japanese and foreign management practices, thus vastly increasing his network of contacts within the Japanese business community).

This cultural element does not have to be Japanese although it is usually more effective when it is, simply because the Japanese can immediately relate to it. One exception worth mentioning was the Texas businessman whose collection of cowboy artifacts—plus his down-to-earth cowboy personality—was sufficiently fascinating to the Japanese to earn him their respect and enthusiastic cooperation in business.

# AND A PINCH OF SEX

As IS OBVIOUS from the size and importance of the mizu shobai in Japan, the sexual attraction between males and females is one of the keys to successful business in Japan.

As camouflaged as it might be, and as different as it might be from the heyday of the legal red-light districts and ubiquitous brothels of pre-1956 Japan, the "water trade" remains a key ingredient in establishing as well as sustaining business relationships in Japan.

For most foreign businessmen, this involves becoming acquainted with the managers of two or three hostess bars where you are welcome and can take Japanese guests, and, if you represent a larger company that can afford the tab, two or three *ryotei* (rio-tay-e), or Japanese style restaurant inns, where geisha can be called in. You may also want to establish "face" at a soapland (hot bath massage parlor).

The managers of most of the smaller, more intimate lounge-type hostess bars where it is best to take Japanese guests are usually women who were formerly hostesses. Given the nature of the business, they are invariably very friendly as well as expert at dealing with men out for a good time.

It is usually necessary to have an introduction to them from a valued Japanese or foreign patron and then to patronize their place on a regular basis over a period of several months to establish the necessary kind of relationship. This means they recognize you by face and name, greet you enthusiastically when you arrive, and allow you to pay your bill by the month if you wish (the Japanese are impressed when a foreigner has established credit at a hostess bar and can walk out without so much as a mention of money).

One of the primary reasons for establishing a personal relationship with hostess bar managers is to make sure the fees you pay are not more than the going rate for regular Japanese patrons. This is very important because generally speaking hostess bars do not operate on the basis of fixed menu prices—which is why I say "fees" instead of "charges." There are generally understood hourly rates for the company of hostesses, and there may be a door or table charge that can be quoted to you. If you ask how much a beer costs, there is usually an answer, but the final bill is not based on what you drank or ate but on how many guests you have in your party, how long you stay in the club, and how many hostesses join your party during your stay, multiplied by the club's base rate for each.

What you should do in advance, if the person who introduced you does not tell you, is ask the manager to give you ballpark figures per guest per hour per hostess.

The variable factor that throws uninitiated foreigners is the system of rotating hostesses among the tables. If you do not establish a limit, a dozen or more may alternately join your party for fifteen or twenty minutes each, running your bill up to astonishing heights In the more unscrupulous places this is often done deliberately, with each hostess being credited with an hour's time even though she may be at your table for just a few minutes.

Foreigners who are new to Japan's mizu shobai system and wander into hostess bar-lounges on their own without settling on a fee in advance are frequently overcharged by a factor of five to ten.

Japan's ryotei, which are what foreigners have traditionally described as "geisha houses," are in fact very private and very exclusive Japanese-style inns—with the traditional tatami floors and sliding paper doors—that serve meals in private rooms and call in geisha for patrons who want their services.

Ryotei are generally not open to the walk-in public. You must have reservations, and in the more prestigious places you must have an introduction from a known and approved patron and make your reservations well in advance. (Exceptions to this are ryotei located in international hotels. They operate like ordinary restaurants—but are two or three times more expensive!)

Neither the hostess bar nor the typical ryotei engage in outright sex for sale. The geisha, especially, are almost never available as sex partners except to well-established patrons.

Again, high-ranking Japanese executives, bureaucrats, and politicians almost always limit their night time excursions to geisha inns, private clubs, and very exclusive restaurants.

# WHEN THE GOING GETS TOUGH

THE TYPICAL foreigner going into his first relationship with a Japanese company is apt to sigh with relief and lower his guard once a contract is signed. That is often premature. The Japanese do not regard a contract as something that is chiseled in stone to be followed precisely to the letter.

A contract in the Japanese sense is an agreement to work together. Of course, there may be provisions that are clearly meant to be followed exactly, but in general they see contracts as guidelines, with a lot of flexibility regardless of the small print.

This attitude goes back to the basic fact that the Japanese do not see things as black or white or absolutely wrong or right. They see things in many shades and believe that it is right and proper to change both their attitudes and behavior with circumstances.

This is why prominent Japanese critics frequently say they do not have principles, they have policies. It is also why so many "right-or-wrong" Westerners are often confused by Japanese behavior and have difficulty understanding them. As a result of this cultural difference, foreigners often encounter more problems with their Japanese partners after contracts have been signed than before—especially when the relationships are intimate ones, in Japan, and require daily contact and regular decisions.

Invariably there will be differences of judgment on what should be done as well as how to do it. One side has to give in or a compromise has to be worked out.

The relationship may work well enough and even exceptionally well when the synergy between the two parties happens to mesh and become more than the sum of one plus one. But the possibility of the relationship becoming a power struggle is more likely. In that case, whether or not the relationship succeeds is determined by the caliber of the managers on both sides.

Overall, management must be wise enough to recognize the sources of friction and, like the judo master, use the weight, energy, and strength of each side to move the project forward despite any differences.

Obviously circumstances do change, often on a daily basis, and it is up to the foreign side to recognize that the Japanese rationale may be just as valid as their own—if not more so—and be prepared to accommodate themselves to it. At the same time, a warning is in order.

The person whose actions are based on policies instead of principles frequently has an advantage over the person of principle. The person of policy can change his actions to give him an advantage, while the person of principle would be prevented from making similar changes.

In the past Japan as a nation, and individual Japanese as well, have often given policy precedence over principle (as most nations and people frequently do), and certainly not always for selfish or unfair or insidious reasons. But the practice is woven deep in the fabric of Japanese culture, and in day-to-day business (or political) affairs with others who play according to different rules, the advantage can tilt the game in their favor.

Follow-up after a contract is signed is just as critically important as during the getting acquainted and negotiating processes and often requires more expertise and persistence because the Japanese participants were on their best behavior during the initial negotiating phase.

191

# WHY THE JAPANESE ARE QUALITY CONSCIOUS

UNTIL the 1970s Japanese business-men and politicians often commented that they learned quality control from the Americans (and then turned the tables on them by doing it better). It is true that the principles of statistical quality control in manufacturing were introduced into Japan shortly after the end of World War II by Dr. W. E. Deming (who was totally ignored by American businessmen until the mid-1980s), and a further significant contribution was made by Dr. J. M. Juran in 1954.

But it was not as if the Japanese were starting from scratch in quality consciousness. The reputation that the Japanese had prior to World War II and in the first decade and a half following the end of the war was a historical fluke that resulted from the demands of foreign importers—not the inclinations or habits of Japanese manufacturers or exporters.

Soon after the U.S. forced feudal Japan to open its doors to the Western world in the 1850s, and following the downfall of the last shogunate dynasty in 1868, large numbers of foreign importers began flocking to Japan with their product samples to place orders for a variety of consumer goods, ranging from toys to textiles.

These foreign buyers were attracted to Japan because labor was cheap and because the Japanese were diligent workers and highly skilled in duplicating samples brought to them by American and European importers.

By the early 1900s the Japanese had the reputation of being the greatest copiers and imitators in the world. They could and would copy anything foreign importers brought to them. Very little of this imitation foreign merchandise was sold in Japan, however. They regarded it with contempt—as something only unsophisticated, uncultured foreigners would buy—and referred to it derisively as *Yokohama hin* (Yokohama heen), or "Yokohama goods," since most of it was shipped out of Japan through the port of Yokohama.

As soon as World War II ended in 1945, foreign importers once again began clamoring to get back into Japan. By the early 1950s, Japan's hotels were bulging at the seams with American and European buyers loaded down with samples they wanted copied in Japan.

Most of these bargain-hunting buyers were from New York City. By 1958 all of the major American department store chains had buying offices in Tokyo or Osaka. The Sears Roebuck buying office in Tokyo alone had a staff of more than sixty people.

The system was simple. Foreign buyers would carry in samples of products they wanted copied in Japan and bring as much pressure as possible on Japanese manufacturers to get the lowest prices possible. The Japanese were hungry and had no choice if they wanted to survive.

Thus for about ten years foreign importers controlled most of what was produced in Japan—its quality as well as its price. Gradually during the last half of the 1950s and then with a rush in the early 1960s, the Japanese began to take control of their export industries. They began coming up with product designs of their own, establishing their own network of buyers abroad, raising the quality level of their merchandise, and resisting the blandishments of foreign importers to continue making cheap imitations.

As they became stronger, Japanese manufacturers began opening sales offices abroad, bypassing not only Japanese exporters but their American and European importers as well. Within a span of about five years Sony and dozens of other soon-to-be-famous Japanese companies broke with their foreign distributors and set up their own networks in the U.S. and elsewhere.

By the 1970s most of the Japanese merchandise being imported into the United States and Europe was not being imported by American or European companies. It was being imported by branch offices of Japanese companies. And the quality of Japanese-made products was widely regarded as the best in the world.

The Japanese were no strangers to quality products. They had a history of nearly two thousand years during which their appreciation of beauty in design and workmanship and their skill as craftsmen were honed to a level seldom reached and never surpassed in any other country.

Their master-apprentice system in the handicrafts and arts produced one generation after another of some of the finest artists and craftsmen in the world. The appreciation of beauty in the ordinary products of life became a cult.

This tradition was ignored by the waves of foreign traders who descended upon Japan from the

195

1860s to the 1960s, but the Japanese were to have their day. One of the many challenges now facing most of the rest of the world is how to compete with Japan in both quality and productivity.

An appreciation for quality is deeply ingrained in Japanese culture and is not something that can be easily imitated. It is a fundamental thing that goes to the root of their values and lifestyle—and is most clearly expressed in the term *kaizen* (kigh-zen).

# THE KAIZEN FACTOR

THE JAPANESE obsession with quality is incorporated in the traditional concept and practice known as kaizen, which can be translated directly as "innovation/goodness" and refers to changes that are desirable. The word is old, going back nearly two millennia to when Japan began importing Chinese arts and crafts and the master-apprentice approach that the Chinese had institutionalized several millennia earlier.

The Japanese took the master-apprentice approach even further than the Chinese, making it an integral part of their culture. It became the philosophy of Japanese artists and craftsman that there was no such thing as "good enough." The ultimate goal was absolute perfection, which meant striving continuously to improve the quality of everything they made. Quality took on a cult-like status.

In the decade following the end of World War II in 1945 the Japanese married the concept of kaizen with the imported statistical control of quality in assembly-line manufacturing—an approach that soon came to be known as "continuous improvement."

The rest, as the saying goes, is history.

It was not until the 1970s, when it appeared that Japan was going to economically colonize the world, that foreign manufacturers began to pick up on the term kaizen and all that it meant. It was to be more than a decade before the introduction of the kaizen concept began to gain a foothold in the U.S.

*This writer introduced the concept of kaizen to the Western world in the late 1950s, first in* The Importer, *a trade magazine published in Tokyo, and then in books, beginning with* Japanese Etiquette & Ethics in Business, *published in 1959. But the concept was generally ignored by American manufacturers until the mid-1970s.*

# THE ART OF SERVICING CUSTOMERS

CUSTOMER SERVICE is another area in which the Japanese are superior to most other people and is one more key that must be on the ring of anyone wanting to succeed in business in Japan.

The Japanese traditions of customer service, like most other aspects of their outlook and behavior, are deeply rooted in their culture. From the beginning of their history down to modern times, Japanese society was based on a finely tuned hierarchical structure of superiors and inferiors. People were divided into highly distinguishable classes and ranks within classes, and there was a very specific and very harshly enforced etiquette for each class and rank.

The behavior of inferiors toward superiors was prescribed. The higher the personage in class and rank, the more precise the behavior and the more carefully it was designed to exalt the superior person. Given human nature, higher-ranking individuals got used to being effusively catered to by underlings, who in turned were conditioned to provide the kind of service expected and demanded.

Over the centuries the concept and practice of a highly refined and stylized form of service gradually permeated Japanese society from top to bottom. Eventually all guests were treated in the same or similar manner as high-ranking superiors. Finally, it became the rule for customers as well to be given the royal treatment. In fact, it became the custom to refer to customers as *O-kyaku San* (Oh-kyack Sahn) or "Mr. (or Mrs.) Honorable Guest."

While considerably diluted in present-day Japan, the age-old custom of treating customers as honored guests is still the bedrock of customer service and is a vitally important aspect of business management. It is expected and typical of Japanese retail shops, wholesalers, and manufacturers that they provide a conspicuously high degree and quality of before-and-after service to their customers—in some cases to an extent that amazes foreigners.

Not surprisingly, the foreigner wanting to succeed in Japan must provide the kind and quality of service consumers naturally expect.

# PUTTING ON A LOVING FACE

ANOTHER facet of Japanese behavior that is especially conspicuous in business, particularly on the retail-consumer level, is one that is called *aiso* (aye-so), which might be translated as "loving care." Aiso refers to a person's facial expression and overall manner.

The Japanese not only demand good service when they go into a store, restaurant, or other place of business, they want a "loving care" expression and manner from the people who wait on them.

Anyone who has been to Japan has witnessed—and heard—innumerable times the reaction of restaurant staff and others in the consumer market when customers come in and leave. Not everyone manages to have loving care smiles on their faces all the time, but the enthusiastic welcomes to arriving customers and expressions of gratitude to department customers make up for it.

This is an established part of the Japanese concept of service, and one they point to with pride when listing all the areas in which Japan is superior to other countries. Of course, much of this kind of behavior is just good sense—having a pleasant look on your face when customers come in, greeting them enthusiastically, and then thanking them profusely when they leave are just good public relations.

But again it is polished to a high art in Japan, and when the Japanese don't receive this kind of treatment, they feel ignored and unappreciated.

Some foreigners who have set up retail businesses in Japan have pooh-poohed this practice when they first started. Most soon learned the wisdom of giving the customers what they want.

# GRINDING SESAME SEEDS

THE FOREIGNER who wants to succeed in doing business with the Japanese should know all about and become an expert at *goma suri* (go-mah suu-ree), which literally means "grinding sesame seeds."

In old Japan, grinding sesame seeds was an unending chore, requiring continuous effort to turn them into a smooth paste.

This term describes a technique the Japanese have developed to maintain harmonious personal relations in spite of the formal, demanding nature of their etiquette. It refers to the unending effort necessary to keep relations with associates, partners, coworkers, and clients smooth and professional. There are so many rules of conduct and people tend to be so sensitive to slights, that most Japanese must spend a significant proportion of their time involved in goma suri.

Probably the most used tools in the goma suri process are compliments and praise, among themselves as well as to foreigners. In fact, foreigners come in for an exceptional amount of praise in Japan because of a strong Japanese desire to appear friendly.

203

Demonstrating the slightest ability with chopsticks or using a few words or sentences of Japanese is invariably enough to elicit effusive compliments.

Responding with proper humility to this kind of behavior and using it at appropriate times will help smooth your way in that you will be going with the flow instead of against it.

A word of caution: in a company situation, paying compliments to young women whom you have just met or know only casually can be taken far more seriously than you might intend. It is best to pay such compliments in private or very discreetly. As is very obvious, the Japanese have no taboos against courtship. But such fun is strictly relegated to its place outside of the office.

# MAKING HAY IN THE
# JAPANESE MARKET

**S**UCCESSFULLY marketing a product in Japan can be both difficult and expensive. Among the reasons for this are the fact that advertising and marketing services tend to be more expensive, the large number and numerous levels of distributors and wholesalers create a maze-like barrier that adds to the cost, and the huge number of retail outlets—over 1.5 million—present both an extraordinary potential and a formidable obstacle.

But in many ways the biggest barrier of all is the Japanese consumer. The Japanese are probably the world's most discriminating and demanding consumers and are surely the best informed. They expect and demand quality down to a minute level. A shirt with a piece of thread hanging out is not acceptable. A product on which the inside or underside is not as perfectly finished as the outside is regarded as a reject. A badly designed product is not likely to go anywhere unless it is sorely needed and there is no other choice—and the Japanese recognize good and bad design when they see it.

Another Japanese trait that throws many foreign companies wanting to market their goods in Japan is their insistence on high-quality packaging. One might be tempted to call them spoiled, but for a thousand years or more packaging in Japan has been an art form, getting as much attention as the products themselves. Japanese businessmen surely spend a larger amount on professional package design than anyone else, and it shows.

To compete in the Japanese market the foreign product generally has to be both designed for and specifically packaged for the market. The publicity and promotion must be carefully crafted to appeal to the subtle, sophisticated tastes of the Japanese, with all the currently sanctioned nuances right on.

Keys to entering the Japanese consumer market successfully include thorough research up front, especially becoming familiar with the distribution and retailing systems in your product area, obtaining copious input and direction from locally recognized, recommended experts, and obtaining the services of a thoroughly experienced Japanese manager.

# GOING AFTER THE YOUNG

IF THERE WERE one general rule that foreigners should follow in their efforts to penetrate the Japanese market, it would be "go after the young." The youth of Japan—from infants to those in their mid-20s—constitute one of the richest and most exciting markets in the world.

Social surveys show that the attitudes and behavior of Japan's urban young—those born after 1965—are so different from what is generally perceived as "Japanese" behavior that they are indeed a "new breed," as they have been labeled by Japanese sociologists.

To succeed in the market of the young requires an intimate knowledge of their lifestyles and the forces that are leading them—fashions, new foods, recreation, and entertainment—and this is one area where foreigners have an advantage over their Japanese counterparts, if they will pick up on it.

The new kind of consumer that Japan's youth have become and are becoming is strictly Western, and American in particular. More and more, they are looking like and acting like Americans, responding to the same motivations

207

and advertising appeals. So drastic are the changes in Japan's "new breed" that older Japanese businessmen can no longer stay on top of the market using their bellies, the universal mind, or any form of traditional cultural wisdom.

The days when Japan's manufacturers could depend on the homogeneity and predictability of the youth segment of the market and do no product research at all are long gone. American and European marketers, with their decades of experience in the volatile youth field, have a definite edge over the old-line Japanese firms that have traditionally dominated the home market and should take advantage of it.

Tokyo marketing consultant/sociologist Dr. Jeanne Binstock has noted that the youth of Japan are more interested in communication than in tranquility, that they want action and richness in their lives, that they want personal achievement, and that they have become "perfect consumers."

For *additional insights into the business and social mind-set of the Japanese, see the author's* Japan's Cultural Code Words—233 Key Terms That Explain the Attitudes and Behavior of the Japanese *and* Kata: The Key to Understanding and Dealing with the Japanese (*both available from Tuttle Publishing*).

# ABOUT THE AUTHOR

B OYÉ LAFAYETTE DE MENTE has been involved with Japan as a student, journalist, and editor since 1949. He is the author of more than thirty books on Japan, China, and Korea. His first book, *Japanese Etiquette & Ethics in Business*, was a pioneer in its field and became an instant bestseller. His other bestsellers include *Asian Face Reading* and *Bachelor's Japan*, which sold over 200,000 copies worldwide. Besides writing, De Mente now works as a business consultant in Asia.

# BOOKS BY
# BOYÉ LAFAYETTE DE MENTE

Asian Face Reading
Chinese Etiquette & Ethics in Business
The Chinese Have a Word for It
Chinese in Plain English
Discovering Cultural Japan
Etiquette Guide to Japan
Instant Chinese
Instant Japanese: Everything You Need in 100 Key Words
Instant Korean
Japanese Business Dictionary
Japanese Etiquette & Ethics in Business
The Japanese Have a Word for It
Japanese Influence on America
Japanese in Plain English
Japan Made Easy—All You Need to Know to Enjoy Japan
Japan's Cultural Code Words
Kata: The Key to Understanding and Dealing with the Japanese
Korean Etiquette & Ethics in Business
Korean in Plain English
Korea's Business and Cultural Code Words
Shoppers Guide to Japan
Subway Guide to Tokyo
Survival Japanese

213